Prediabetes Cookbook 2021

The Ultimate Guide for Beginners with Easy and Delicious Prediabetes Diet Recipes. (Diabetic Recipe Book)

Sarah Jones

Table of Contents

Hey there!

I would like to thank you for your trust and I really hope you'll enjoy the book.

A lot of thought and effort went into creating the book. I am not a part of a big publishing company and I take care of the whole publishing process myself in an effort to make sure your cooking journey is as smooth as possible.

If for any reason you did not like the book you can write on my email at deliciousrecipes.publishing@gmail.com. I always make sure to get back to everybody and if you're not happy with the book I can share another book.

I'm trying really hard to create the best cookbooks I can and I'm always open to constructive criticism.

Enjoy!

What Is Prediabetes?

Prediabetes indicates that you are at risk of diabetes, and that steps need to be taken to reduce your chances of becoming diabetic. Making changes to your lifestyle and diet can help to prevent diabetes entirely at this stage, but quick action needs to be taken.

We will cover prediabetes in more detail in a later chapter, but a diagnosis of prediabetes should not be ignored. At this stage, your chances of reducing your glucose levels and preventing the development of diabetes are reasonably high provided you make positive changes, so take the diagnosis very seriously.

Symptoms And Warning Signs Of Prediabetes

So, how do you know if you might be suffering from prediabetes? You might wonder what symptoms you should look out for if you are concerned about this, but unfortunately, it is common for no symptoms to show up at all. It is thought that up to 90% of people who suffer from prediabetes do not know that they have it at all. Adults over 45 should be screened for prediabetes every few years, particularly if they are overweight and therefore at greater risk of developing the condition.

However, it is possible that you may experience some symptoms, and if you do, you should request a check-up from your doctor. Common symptoms include blurry vision, an increased need to urinate, increased thirst, tiredness, and blurred vision. Any of these may occur, or you may experience none of them. Some people do not experience these symptoms even once the condition has progressed to type 2 diabetes.

Because there are not necessarily any warning signs of prediabetes, it is important to get checked reasonably often and to manage your weight and diet as best you can.

Healthy Habits and Actions You Can Take

It is not possible to cure prediabetes, but it is possible to reverse it. Discuss potential treatments with your doctor, and also review the suggested actions above, as these will help you to manage prediabetes as well as diabetes.

Exercising and eating well are the keys to managing and undoing this condition. As mentioned, eating fewer simple carbohydrates, more vegetables, lean meats, and whole grains is a good starting point. Losing excess weight is also important. If you are a smoker, you should aim to stop smoking quickly as smoking has been connected with insulin resistance and type 2 diabetes.

Careful management, coupled with medication if necessary, will help to reverse prediabetes, although you will need to continue these good practices going forward.

What Glucose Level Is Considered As Prediabetes?

To diagnose prediabetes, your doctor will probably do an A1C test, and a reading between 5.7% and 6.4% is considered prediabetes. If your level is higher than 6.5%, you will usually be asked to do a second test, and if this shows the same level, you are likely suffering from type 2 diabetes.

How Long Does It Take To Go From Prediabetes To Diabetes?

This can vary enormously depending on your diet, overall health, and lifestyle. Some people will never develop diabetes even though they have prediabetes. Some people will develop diabetes very quickly. Currently, around a quarter of people diagnosed with prediabetes will progress to type 2 diabetes in less than five years.

Remember that a diagnosis of prediabetes is not a sure sign that you will get type 2 diabetes in X amount of years. If you take a proactive approach, you may be able to reverse your condition, or at least stave off diabetes for very many more years. It is important to take up regular exercise and improve your diet, as well as lose a little weight (at least for most people; it is possible to develop prediabetes and diabetes even if you are not overweight).

Take a diagnosis of prediabetes as a sign that you need to change your lifestyle and improve your health, not as a certainty that you will develop diabetes in just a few years.

What Foods Should You Avoid If You Are Prediabetic?

It probably won't surprise you to learn that there is a lot of overlap in the foods you should avoid as a prediabetic and foods you should avoid as a diabetic. Here are some of the top foods you should take off your menu, or severely limit going forwards:

- Fried foods, e.g. doughnuts, fried chicken, **chips**, etc.

- Sweetened low-fat products, such as yogurt

- Alcohol

- Fruit juice

- Dried fruit

- High-starch vegetables, such as corn and sweet potatoes

- Sweet drinks

- Crisps

- Processed grains

- High sugar snacks, e.g. chocolate, cake, ice cream, pastries, etc.

If you do consume things from this list, bear in mind that it is important to combine them with proteins to reduce the impact of the sugar on your system. Try to balance any "cheats" you have with healthy eating to reduce the overall impact.

Management and Nutritional Adjustments

Exercise: if you are diagnosed with prediabetes, you will immediately want to focus upon your diet, your weight, and your exercise routine (or lack thereof). We'll discuss the exercise routine first.

If you don't exercise at all, you need to begin doing so, but it is important to start out slowly. Your body will not be used to exercising and if you do too much to begin with, you're likely to overwhelm your body and put yourself off exercising for good. Try to choose an exercise you think you can enjoy. If you like running, try going for a regular jog.

If you already exercise a bit, you may already have an idea of how to start, but you should still be cautious about doing too much too quickly. You might be keen to beat back the condition as fast as possible, but a slow and steady approach is better.

Try to increase your exercise days by one or two per week to begin with, and just add another ten minutes to each session. This can make a big difference without feeling impossible. It is a good idea to vary your exercises if you can so that you work out different muscles and reduce your risk of injury.

Turn to others to help motivate you if you're finding it hard to get going or stay focused. You might be able to find someone who will go on a run with you some days of the week, or you could join a running club. You might also consider talking to personal fitness trainers or joining a gym.

Medication: You should discuss a treatment plan with your doctor, and take on board their suggestions about medicating or not medicating. The question of whether to medicate prediabetes or not tends to be controversial, and many doctors believe that exercise and diet changes remain the optimal treatment for prediabetes. These are habit-forming and more effective in the long term than many medications, and won't produce unpleasant side effects.

However, your doctor may decide that medication is right in your circumstances. This should be used in conjunction with exercise and improved eating. At present, Metformin is the only medication that the American Diabetes Association recommends for the treatment of prediabetes. This is usually given to the highest risk individuals. Don't insist on medication if your doctor would prefer to try other changes first, as it is only a partial solution to the condition.

Blood Sugar Management: Other management steps that you need to take include measuring your blood sugar. You may be given a blood sugar meter to use at home. This will use a small drop of your blood and test the sugar levels. You can also use a continuous glucose monitor to measure your blood sugar.

Your doctor will tell you how frequently you should test it; try to set reminders so that you don't miss check-ups. The more information you have about your blood sugar levels, the more easily you and your doctor will be able to handle your condition.

Nutritional Adjustments: One of the most important aspects of managing prediabetes is your diet. You are going to need to reduce the number of simple carbohydrates and the amount of sugar that you consume. You may find that it helps to talk to others who suffer from the condition. Collect some go-to recipes that are tailored to your needs and start to incorporate these into your diet.

You do not need to make changes all at once, but bear in mind that your prediabetes can quickly progress, and you need to slow it down as much as possible. If you already use a meal plan, adjust it to include new recipes most days, and if you don't use a meal plan, consider starting one.

Use the list of approved foods, the glycemic index, the foods you should avoid, and the general rules of thumb (e.g. avoid simple carbohydrates) to build a meal plan that will work for you. You can probably find a template and many other suggestions online. Begin working this into your daily routine and stick to it as much as you can.

Over time, you should see your weight start to decrease and your overall blood sugar levels fall. Remember, it is important to be vigilant and stick to your diet even once you have achieved this. Too many sweets and simple carbohydrates could see your blood sugar level averages climbing once more.

Give Up Smoking If You Smoke: Smoking increases your risk of diabetes, and quitting has some major benefits for your overall health as well as your health in relation to prediabetes. However, this comes with a caveat. It has recently been found that giving up smoking can cause an increase in your blood sugar levels for around three years. It looks as though your glycemic control temporarily drops when you first quit, and it takes time for these levels to rebalance themselves.

Although the study accounted for this, it is true that quitting smoking can lead to cravings, which could push your blood sugar up and increase your stress levels. Smoking is an appetite suppressant and if you stop, you may find that you gain weight even if you try and stick to your healthy meal plans.

However, it is still advised that you attempt to quit smoking if you are a smoker who is suffering from prediabetes. The long-term gains outweigh the short-term issues. You should discuss a plan with your doctor, taking into account the potential rise in blood sugar levels, and ensure that you are taking the right steps going forward.

Measurement Conversions

It is important to note that it is virtually impossible to include an all-inclusive conversion table as all foods have slightly different measurements when converted.

KITCHEN CONVERSIONS

LIQUID CONVERSIONS

1/4 TSP	= 1 ML		
1/2 TSP	= 2 ML		
1 TSP	= 5 ML		
3 TSP	= 1 TBL	= 1/2 FL OZ	= 15 ML
2 TBLS	= 1/8 CUP	= 1 FL OZ	= 30 ML
4 TBLS	= 1/4 CUP	= 2 FL OZ	= 60 ML
5 1/3 TBLS	= 1/3 CUP	= 3 FL OZ	= 80 ML
8 TBLS	= 1/2 CUP	= 4 FL OZ	= 120 ML
10 2/3	= 2/3 CUP	= 5 FL OZ	= 160 ML
12 TBLS	= 3/4 CUP	= 6 FL OZ	= 180 ML
16 TBLS	= 1 CUP	= 8 FL OZ	= 240 ML
1 PT	= 2 CUPS	= 16 FL OZ	= 480 ML
1 QT	= 4 CUPS	= 32 FL OZ	= 960 ML
33 FL OZ	= 1000 ML	= 1 L	

Length

METRIC	IMPERIAL
3mm	1/8 inch
6mm	1/4 inch
2.5cm	1 inch
3cm	1 1/4 inch
5cm	2 inches
10cm	4 inches
15cm	6 inches
20cm	8 inches
22.5cm	9 inches
25cm	10 inches
28cm	11 inches

Oven Temperatures

	Fahrenheit	Celsius	Gas Mark
Freezing Water	32°F	0°C	
Room Temp.	68°F	20°C	
Boiling Water	212° F	100°C	
Baking	325° F	160°C	3
	350° F	180°C	4
	375° F	190°C	5
	400° F	200°C	6
	425° F	220°C	7
	450° F	230°C	8
Broiling			Grill

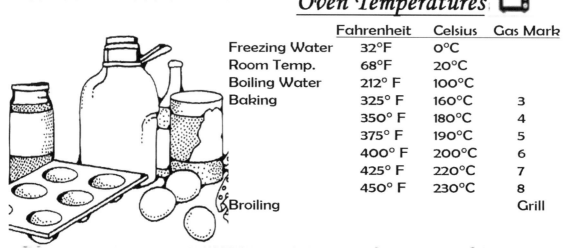

Weight Conversions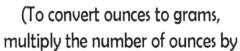

(To convert ounces to grams, multiply the number of ounces by 30.)

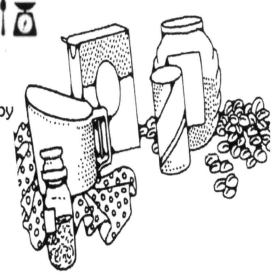

1 oz	=	1/16 lb	=	30 g
4 oz	=	1/4 lb	=	120 g
8 oz	=	1/2 lb	=	240 g
12 oz	=	3/4 lb	=	360 g
16 oz	=	1 lb	=	480 g

Conversions for Different Types of Food

Standard Cup	Fine Powder (like flour)	Grains (like rice)	Granular (like sugar)	Liquid Solids (like butter)	Liquid (eg. milk)
1	140 g	150 g	190 g	200 g	240 ml
3/4	105 g	113 g	143 g	150 g	180 ml
2/3	93 g	100 g	125 g	133 g	160 ml
1/2	70 g	75 g	95 g	100 g	120 ml
1/3	47 g	50 g	63 g	67 g	80 ml
1/4	35 g	38 g	48 g	50 g	60 ml
1/8	18 g	19 g	24 g	25 g	30 ml

Breakfast Recipes

Kickstart Your Day Berry Smoothie

Servings| 2   Time| 20 minutes
Nutritional Content (per serving):
Cal| 260   Fat| 29 g   Protein| 15 g   Carbs| 7 g

Ingredients:
- ❖ 2 orange
- ❖ 285 grams Greek yogurt
- ❖ 2 Bananas small, peeled
- ❖ 650 grams strawberries
- ❖ 2 tbsp flaxseeds

Directions:
1. Cut the orange in half and remove the pit. Cube the pulp.
2. Place the ingredients in a food processor. Process until the ingredients are combined.
3. Serve immediately, or chill for an hour before serving.

Avocado and Goat Cheese Toast

Servings| 2   Time| 5 minutes
Nutritional Content (per serving):
Cal| 137   Fat| 6 g   Protein| 5 g   Carbs| 18 g

Ingredients:
- ❖ 2 Whole-wheat thin-sliced bread
- ❖ Half of avocado
- ❖ 2 tbsp goat cheese
- ❖ Salt (to taste)

Directions:

1. In a toaster or broiler, toast the bread until browned.
2. Remove the flesh from the avocado. In a medium bowl, use a fork to mash the avocado flesh. Use it to spread onto your toast.
3. To with a sprinkle of goat cheese and season to taste.
4. Add any toppings and serve.

Buckwheat Pancakes

Servings| 2   Time| 30 minutes
Nutritional Content (per serving):
Cal| 657   Fat| 29 g   Protein| 15 g   Carbs| 110 g

Ingredients:
- 2 Egg
- 1/2 tsp baking soda
- 2 tsp baking powder
- 625 ml Buttermilk
- 280 grams buckwheat flour
- 30 ml honey
- 7 ml vanilla extract
- Salt (pinch)
- 30 grams clarified ghee

Directions:
1. Mix in a bowl, buckwheat flour, baking powder, soda, salt, and honey.
2. In a separate bowl, add all wet ingredients and whisk together.
3. Combine dry and wet ingredients to form a thick, smooth batter. Let it rest for 15 minutes.
4. Heat a skillet and add some olive oil.
5. In the centre of the skillet, pour a large spoonful of batter a few inches in diameter and less than an inch in thickness.
6. When the batter starts bubbling over. This indicates it is time to flip it.
7. Flip the pancake and cook on both sides, pouring some more olive oil if needed to prevent sticking.
8. Pancake is done once it is brown, in about 2-3 minutes. Repeat these steps for the remaining batter.
9. Serve the pancakes warm with honey, fruit, or honey.

Couscous

Servings| 5   Time| 35 minutes
Nutritional Content (per serving):
Cal| 426   Fat| 11 g   Protein| 21 g   Carbs| 62 g

Ingredients:

- ❖ 450 grams uncooked whole-wheat couscous
- ❖ 2 L skim milk
- ❖ 3 5 cm cinnamon stick
- ❖ 90 ml honey
- ❖ pinch of salt
- ❖ 60 ml olive oil
- ❖ 120 grams raisins and currants
- ❖ 350 grams dried apricots

Directions:

1. In a medium pan, combine cinnamon and milk and let boil for 3 minutes, stirring constantly.
2. Remove from heat; add the couscous, dried fruits, currants and salt, and 4 tsp of honey to the pan. Mix well.
3. Cover and set aside for 15 minutes.
4. Pour into 4 serving bowls and add 1 tsp olive oil and ½ tsp honey on top of each bowl. Stir and serve immediately.

Gluten-Free Carrot and Oat Pancakes

Servings|4   Time| 30 minutes
Nutritional Content (per serving):
Cal| 257   Fat| 9 g   Protein| 15 g   Carbs| 24 g

Ingredients:

- ❖ 90 grams rolled oats
- ❖ 230 grams shredded carrots
- ❖ 200 grams low-fat cottage cheese
- ❖ 2 eggs
- ❖ 110 ml almond milk
- ❖ 1 tsp. baking powder

- ❖ ½ tsp ground cinnamon
- ❖ 2 tbsp. ground flaxseed
- ❖ 80 grams greek yogurt
- ❖ 1 tbsp pure honey
- ❖ 2 tsp., divided canola oil

Directions:

1. In a blender jar, process the oats until they resemble flour. Add the carrots, cottage cheese, eggs, almond milk, baking powder, cinnamon, and flaxseed to the jar. Process until smooth.
2. In a small bowl, combine the yogurt and honey and stir well. Set aside.
3. In a large skillet, heat 1 teaspoon of oil over medium heat. Using a measuring cup, add ⅔ dl of batter per pancake to the skillet.
4. Cook for 1 to 2 minutes until bubbles form on the surface and flip the pancakes.
5. Cook for another minute until the pancakes are browned and cooked through.
6. Repeat with the remaining 1 teaspoon of oil and remaining batter. Serve warm topped with the honey yogurt.

Oatmeal with Fruits & Nuts

Servings| 5   Time| 30 minutes
Nutritional Content (per serving):
Cal| 211   Fat| 1 g   Protein| 10 g   Carbs| 40 g

Ingredients:
- 600 grams, raw oats
- 1.2 L skim milk or water
- 1 ¼ tsp cinnamon
- 1, chopped peach
- Handful of raisins
- 300 grams dried cranberries
- Assorted nuts, blanched and slivered to sprinkle on top
- 2 ½ tsp honey (optional)

Directions:
1. Cook the oats as per instructions then add the remaining ingredients.
2. Add seasonal fruits and nuts to enhance the flavour of the oatmeal.
3. Add blueberries, strawberries, and honey for a more classic combination. Enjoy!

Greek Yogurt Bowl

Servings| 2   Time| 15 minutes
Nutritional Content (per serving):
Cal| 387   Fat| 9 g   Protein| 10 g   Carbs| 76 g

Ingredients:
- 400 grams, plain greek yogurt
- 230 grams raspberries
- 6, hulled and sliced strawberries
- 200 grams, fresh blueberries
- 4 tbsp, raw organic honey

Directions:
1. Place Greek yogurt in a bowl. Add the sliced banana and berries.
2. Drizzle honey on top. Top with seeds and nuts of your choice (if desired).
3. Serve chilled.

Mediterranean Omelette with Wheat Bread & Blueberries

Servings| 2   Time| 30 minutes
Nutritional Content (per serving):
Cal| 427   Fat| 35 g   Protein| 9 g   Carbs| 24 g

Ingredients:
- ❖ 4, large eggs
- ❖ 4 tbsp, extra virgin olive oil
- ❖ 2 medium, chopped yellow onion
- ❖ 2 cloves, minced garlic
- ❖ 460 grams spinach
- ❖ 1 medium diced tomato
- ❖ 4 tbsp skim milk
- ❖ 8, pitted and diced kalamata olives
- ❖ Salt and pepper
- ❖ 6 tbsp, crumbled feta cheese
- ❖ 2 tbsp, fresh parsley (chopped)

For Serving:
- ❖ 4 sliced whole wheat bread
- ❖ 220 grams blueberries
- ❖ 400 ml skim milk/coffee

Directions:
1. Heat the oil in a pan. Add onions to the pan and fry until brown. Then, add garlic and fry for 2 minutes.
2. Add the salt, spinach, tomatoes, and cook for a few minutes. In a bowl, add egg and milk and whisk together.
3. Add the pepper and olives to the frying pan and pour the egg mixture over the sautéed vegetables.
4. Spread it around and turn up the heat so the egg cooks quickly.
5. You can lift the omelette a bit to allow the upper liquid layer to go underneath the cooked egg.
6. Continue cooking until the egg is cooked. Fold the omelette in half. Transfer to a plate, add freshly chopped parsley and cheese.
7. Serve warm with 2 slices of Whole Wheat Bread, 1 ⅛ dl Blueberries, and 1 Glass of Milk/Coffee.

Simple Mediterranean Breakfast With Sashimi & Pickles

Servings| 5   Time| 15 minutes
Nutritional Content (per serving):
Cal| 215   Fat| 11 g   Protein| 12 g   Carbs| 18 g

Ingredients:

- ❖ 200 grams, fresh ricotta cheese
- ❖ 430 grams salmon sashimi grade
- ❖ 5 eggs
- ❖ 5 green olives
- ❖ 5 slice sourdough rye bread

- ❖ 15 slices fresh pickles
- ❖ 3 tsp olive oil
- ❖ sea salt and fresh black pepper (to taste)

Directions:
1. Boil your eggs and slice your salmon.
2. Spread the ricotta on the bread, each slice top with a sliced egg, salmon, pickle slices, and an olive.
3. Drizzle with olive oil then seasons with salt and pepper. Enjoy!

Blueberry-Chia Smoothie

Servings | 2   Time| 5 minutes
Nutritional Content (per serving):
Cal| 360   Fat| 16 g   Protein| 12 g   Carbs| 46 g

Ingredients:

- ❖ 330 grams frozen blueberries
- ❖ ½ medium frozen banana
- ❖ 2 tbsp peanut butter
- ❖ 2 tbsp chia seeds
- ❖ 340 grams unsweetened soy milk

Directions:

1. Combine the blueberries banana peanut butter chia seeds and soy milk in a blender
2. and blend on high speed until smooth.
3. Use a spatula - scrape down the sides as needed
4. Serve immediately If it's too thick add more soy milk or water by the tablespoonful until you've reached the desired consistency.

Cherry, Chocolate, and Almond Shake

Servings| 2   Time| 5 minutes
Nutritional Content (per serving):
Cal| 284   Fat| 16 g   Protein| 10 g   Carbs| 32g

Ingredients:

- ❖ 280 grams frozen cherries
- ❖ 2 tbsp cocoa powder
- ❖ 2 tbsp almond butter
- ❖ 2 tbsp hemp seeds
- ❖ 230 grams unsweetened almond milk

Directions:
1. Combine the cherries cocoa almond butter hemp seeds and almond milk in a blender and blend on high speed until smooth
2. Use a spatula - scrape down the sides as needed Serve immediately

Stovetop Granola

Servings| 4 ½ cups   Time| 20 minutes
Nutritional Content (per serving):
Cal| 164   Fat| 11 g   Protein| 4 g   Carbs| 15 g

Ingredients:

- 150 grams rolled oats
- 60 ml vegetable
- 80 grams honey or maple syrup
- 1 tbsp spice
- 1 tbsp citrus zest
- 140 grams roasted chopped nuts
- 100 grams sunflower seeds
- 70 grams golden raisins
- Kosher salt

Directions:

1. Heat a large dry skillet preferably cast iron over medium-high heat Add the grains and cook stirring frequently until golden brown and toasty Remove the grains from the skillet and transfer them - a small bowl
2. Reduce the heat - medium return the skillet to the heat and add the vegetable oil honey and spice Stir until thoroughly combined and bring to a simmer
3. Once the mixture begins - bubble reduce the heat to low and add the citrus zest toasted grains nuts seeds and dried fruit
4. Stir and cook for another 2 minutes or until the granola is sticky and you can smell the spices Adjust the seasonings as desired and add salt to taste
5. Allow the granola - cool before storing it in an airtight container at room temperature for up to 6 months

Seedy Muesli

Servings| 6 cups   Time| 5 minutes
Nutritional Content (per serving):
Cal| 430   Fat| 29 g   Protein| 16 g   Carbs| 30 g

Ingredients:

- 200 grams gluten-free rolled oats
- 115 grams roasted slivered almonds
- 100 grams raw sunflower seeds
- 75 grams raw pumpkin seeds
- 60 grams pistachios
- 95 grams apricots
- 40 grams hemp seeds
- 25 grams ground flaxseed
- 35 grams toasted sesame seeds

Directions:

1. In a medium bowl combine the oats almonds sunflower seeds pumpkin seeds pistachios apricots hemp seeds flaxseed and sesame seeds
2. Store the mixture in an airtight container at room temperature for up - 6 months

Apple Millet Porridge

Servings| 2   Time| 15 minutes
Nutritional Content (per serving):
Cal| 605   Fat| 17 g   Protein| 15 g   Carbs| 102 g

Ingredients:

- ❖ 200 grams millet
- ❖ 590 ml plant-based milk
- ❖ 2 tsp ground cinnamon
- ❖ Pinch kosher salt
- ❖ 1 tbsp honey
- ❖ 1 apple cored and cut into bite-size pieces
- ❖ 30 grams chopped walnuts

Directions:

1. In a small saucepan combine the millet, 500 ml milk, cinnamon and salt and place over medium heat.
2. Cook stirring until the millet puffs up and is fully cooked 10 - 12 minutes
3. Remove the millet from the heat and slowly add the remaining 92 ml milk along with the honey Adjust the seasonings as desired
4. Divide the millet between two bowls and top each with half of the apple and walnuts
5. Store any leftovers in an airtight container in the refrigerator for up - 5 days

Breakfast Banana Barley

Servings| 2   Time| 15 minutes
Nutritional Content (per serving):
Cal| 725   Fat| 14 g   Protein| 21 g   Carbs| 136 g

Ingredients:
- ❖ 710 ml water
- ❖ Pinch kosher salt
- ❖ 135 grams quick barley
- ❖ 3 tbsp natural peanut butter
- ❖ 1 banana sliced

Directions:
1. In a small saucepan, bring the water and salt - a boil over high heat
2. Stir in the barley, cover, reduce the heat, and simmer for 10 minutes or until tender
3. Remove the saucepan from the heat and add the peanut butter, stirring - blend Adjust the salt as desired, and divide the mixture between two bowls
4. Top with the sliced bananas and serve
5. Store any leftovers in an airtight container in the refrigerator for up - 5 days

Harvest Blackberry Quinoa Bowl

Servings| 2   Time| 25 minutes
Nutritional Content (per serving):
Cal| 286   Fat| 3 g   Protein| 10 g   Carbs| 53 g

Ingredients:

- ❖ 355 ml water
- ❖ Pinch kosher salt
- ❖ ¾ cup quinoa

- ❖ 170 grams halved blackberries
- ❖ Ground cinnamon, for garnish

Directions:

1. In a medium saucepan, bring the water and salt - a boil over high heat, reduce the heat to low, and add the quinoa
2. Cook until you see the grains are tender and the liquid is absorbed, about 15 minutes
3. Remove the quinoa from the heat If you prefer your quinoa - be fluffy, then cover with a lid for a few minutes and allow it to rest
4. Once the quinoa is rested, use a fork - fluff it up, top it with the blackberries and a sprinkle of cinnamon, and serve
5. If you like your grains creamier, serve immediately topped with blackberries and cinnamon

High-Protein Oatmeal

Servings| 1   Time| 10 minutes
Nutritional Content (per serving):
Cal| 373   Fat| 13 g   Protein| 15 g   Carbs| 49 g

Ingredients:

- ❖ 225 grams vanilla soy milk
- ❖ 50 grams oats
- ❖ 1 tbsp chia seeds
- ❖ 40 grams blueberries
- ❖ 1 tbsp sliced and toasted almonds

Directions:

1. In a medium saucepan over medium-high heat, stir together the soy milk and oats
2. Bring - a boil, reduce the heat to low, and simmer, stirring frequently, until cooked and tender, 5 - 8 minutes
3. Remove the oatmeal from the heat and serve topped with chia seeds, blueberries, and almonds
4. Store any leftovers in an airtight container in the refrigerator for up - 5 days.

Carrot Cake Oatmeal

Servings| 1   Time| 13 minutes
Nutritional Content (per serving):
Cal| 445   Fat| 21 g   Protein| 21 g   Carbs| 47 g

Ingredients:

- 110 ml unsweetened almond milk
- 120 ml water
- 1 grated carrot
- 30 grams rolled oats
- 1 tbsp golden raisins
- 1 tsp honey
- Pinch ground cinnamon
- 1½ tbsp almond butter
- 100 grams cottage cheese

Directions:

1. In a small saucepan, combine the almond milk, water, grated carrot, oats, golden raisins, honey, and cinnamon over medium heat. Bring the mixture to a boil, reduce the heat to low, and simmer, stirring occasionally, until the oats are cooked, about 7 minutes.
2. Mix in the almond butter, remove the saucepan from the heat, and transfer the oats to a bowl.
3. Serve immediately, topped with cottage cheese.
4. Store any leftovers in an airtight container in the refrigerator for up to 5 days.

Strawberry-Ricotta Toast

Servings| 1   Time| 5 minutes
Nutritional Content (per serving):
Cal| 634   Fat| 30 g   Protein| 25 g   Carbs| 73 g

Ingredients:

- ❖ 2 slices whole-grain bread toasted
- ❖ 125 grams ricotta cheese
- ❖ 335 grams diced strawberries
- ❖ 3 tbsp toasted chopped hazelnuts
- ❖ 2 tbsp chopped fresh mint

Directions:
1. Place the toast on your work surface and evenly divide the ricotta between the slices, spreading it out to cover the bread.
2. Top each slice with the strawberries, hazelnuts, and mint (if using), evenly distributing the ingredients on the cheese.
3. Serve immediately.

Easy Buckwheat Crêpes

Servings| 12   Time| 5 minutes
Nutritional Content (per serving):
Cal| 130   Fat| 5 g   Protein| 5 g   Carbs| 18 g

Ingredients:

- 120 grams buckwheat flour
- 410 ml milk
- ⅛ tsp kosher salt
- 1 tbsp extra-virgin olive oil
- ½ tbsp ground flaxseed

Directions:

1. Combine the buckwheat flour, milk, salt, extra-virgin olive oil, and flaxseed (if using), in a bowl and whisk thoroughly, or in a blender and pulse until well combined.
2. Heat a non-stick medium skillet over medium heat. Once it's hot, add a 62.5 ml of batter to the skillet, spreading it out evenly. Cook until bubbles appear and the edges crisp like a pancake, 1 to 3 minutes, then flip and cook for another 2 minutes.
3. Repeat until all the batter is used up, and the crêpes are cooked. Layer parchment paper or tea towels between the crêpes to keep them from sticking to one another while also keeping them warm until you're ready to eat.
4. Serve with the desired fillings.
5. Store any leftovers in an airtight container in the refrigerator for up to 3 days.

Shakshuka

Servings| 4   Time| 30 minutes
Nutritional Content (per serving):
Cal| 259   Fat| 14 g   Protein| 12 g   Carbs| 22 g

Ingredients:

- ❖ 2 tbsp extra-virgin olive oil
- ❖ 1 diced onion
- ❖ 2 tbsp tomato paste
- ❖ 2 diced red bell peppers
- ❖ 2 tbsp Harissa
- ❖ 4 garlic cloves minced
- ❖ 2 tsp ground cumin

- ❖ ½ tsp ground coriander
- ❖ 1 tsp smoked paprika
- ❖ 2 cans diced tomatoes
- ❖ 4 large eggs
- ❖ 110 grams plain Greek yogurt
- ❖ Bread, for dipping (optional)

Directions:

1. Heat the extra-virgin olive oil in a Dutch oven or large saucepan over medium heat. When it starts to shimmer, add the onion and cook until translucent, about 3 minutes.
2. Add the tomato paste, peppers, harissa (if using), garlic, cumin, coriander (if using), paprika, and tomatoes. Bring to a simmer and cook 10 to 15 minutes, until the peppers are cooked, and the sauce is thick. Adjust the seasoning as desired.
3. Make four wells in the mixture with the back of a large spoon and gently break one egg into each well. Cover the saucepan and simmer gently until the egg whites are set but the yolks are still runny, 5 to 8 minutes.
4. Remove the saucepan from the heat and spoon the tomato mixture and one cooked egg into each of four bowls. Top with the Greek yogurt and serve with bread (if using)

Sides

Black Bean Cake with Salsa

Servings| 20   Time| 35 minutes
Nutritional Content (per serving):
Cal| 257   Fat| 12 g   Protein| 9 g   Carbs| 30 g

Ingredients:
- 30 ml olive oil
- 450 grams onion brunoised
- 3 cloves garlic
- Jalapenos seeded and brunoised
- 2 tsp ground cumin
- 910 grams black beans cooked
- 1 tsp, dried oregano
- Salt (to taste)
- Pepper (to taste)
- 450 ml salsa cruda

Directions:
1. Heat the olive oil in a sauté pan over low heat. Add the garlic and onions, cook until soft. Do not brown.
2. Add the ground cumin and jalapeno. Cook for a few more minutes. Add the oregano and beans. Cook until they are heated through.
3. Place the mixture in a food processor and blend in a puree. The mixture should be thick to hold its shape. If the mixture becomes too dry, moisten with a little water.
4. Adjust the seasoning with salt and pepper if needed. Divide the mixture into 50 g portions. Form into small, flat cakes.
5. Brown the cakes lightly on both sides in hot olive oil in a sauté pan. They will be exceptionally soft; handle carefully.
6. Serve 2 cakes per portion with salsa.

Pickled Apple

Servings| 12   Time| 10 minutes
Nutritional Content (per serving):
Cal| 50   Fat| 0 g   Protein| 0 g   Carbs| 12 g

Ingredients:
- 110 ml water
- 100 grams honey
- 110 grams cider vinegar

Sachet:
- 4 peppercorns
- 1/4 tsp mustard seed
- 1/4 tsp coriander seed
- 1/4 tsp salt
- 2 granny smith apple peeled, cored, and cut into small dice
- 1 tbsp, cut chiffonade italian parsley

Directions:
1. Combine the water, honey, vinegar, sachet, and sat in a saucepan. Bring to a boil.
2. Pour the liquid and the sachet over the apples in a nonreactive container.
3. Let it be refrigerated for 3-4 hours or overnight.
4. Drain the apples before serving and toss with the parsley.

Baked Clams Oreganata

Servings| 10   Time| 45 minutes
Nutritional Content (per serving):
Cal| 180   Fat| 9 g   Protein| 10 g   Carbs| 16 g

Ingredients:
- ❖ 30 cherrystone clams (removed from shell and juices reserved)
- ❖ 60 ml olive oil
- ❖ 30 grams onions (chopped fine)
- ❖ 1 tsp garlic
- ❖ 30 ml lemon juice
- ❖ 280 grams fresh breadcrumbs
- ❖ 1 tbsp parsley chopped
- ❖ 3/4 tsp oregano dried
- ❖ 1/8 tsp white pepper
- ❖ 80 grams parmesan cheese
- ❖ Paprika (as needed)
- ❖ 10 lemon wedges

Directions:
1. Chop the clams into small pieces. Heat the oil in a sauté pan. Add the onion and garlic. Sauté about 1 minute, but do not brown.
2. Use half of the clam juice, then reduce it over high heat by three-fourths.
3. Remove from the heat and add the crumbs, parsley, lemon juice, white pepper, and oregano. Mix gently to avoid making the crumbs pasty.
4. If necessary, adjust the seasonings. Once the mixture has cooled. Mix in the chopped clams.
5. Place the mixture in the 30 clamshells. Sprinkle with paprika and parmesan cheese.
6. Transfer to a sheet pan and refrigerate until needed.
7. For each order, bake 3 clams in a hot oven 230 °C (450 °F) until they are hot and the top brown.
8. Garnish with a lemon wedge.

Tuna Tartare

Servings| 8   Time| 15 minutes
Nutritional Content (per serving):
Cal| 200   Fat| 12 g   Protein| 21 g   Carbs| 2 g

Ingredients:

- 200 grams sashimi quality tuna (well-trimmed)
- 50 grams shallots (minced)
- 2 tbsp parsley (chopped)
- 2 tbsp fresh tarragon (chopped)
- 2 tbsp lime juice
- 30 ml ijon-style mustard
- 70 ml olive oil
- Salt (to tasted)
- White pepper (to taste)

Directions:
1. Use a knife to mince the tuna.
2. Mixed the rest of the ingredients with the chopped tuna before serving. Season to taste with pepper and salt.

Cod Cakes

Servings| 12   Time| 60 minutes
Nutritional Content (per serving):
Cal| 280   Fat| 6 g   Protein| 23 g   Carbs| 33 g

Ingredients:

- 340 grams cod cooked
- 340 grams turnips puree
- 2 whole eggs beaten
- 1 egg yolk beaten
- Salt (to taste)
- White pepper (to taste)

- pinch ground ginger
Standard Breading Procedure:
- Whole wheat flour (as needed)
- Egg wash (as needed)
- Breadcrumbs (as needed)
- Tomatoes sauce (as desired)

Directions:
1. Flake the fish until it is well shredded. Combine with the turnips, egg, and egg yolk.
2. Season to taste with salt, pepper, and a little ground ginger. Scale the mixture into 70 grams portions.
3. Shape the mixture into a ball then slightly flattened the mixture cakes.
4. Put the mixture through the Standard Breading Procedure. Deep-fry at 180 °C until golden brown.
5. Serve 2 cakes per portion. Accompany with tomato sauce.

Grilled Vegetable Kebabs

Servings| 12   Time| 30 minutes
Nutritional Content (per serving):
Cal| 50   Fat| 3 g   Protein| 18 g   Carbs| 5 g

Ingredients:
- 170 grams zucchini (trimmed)
- 170 grams yellow Summer Squash (trimmed)
- 170 grams bell pepper red or orange, cut into 4 cm. squares
- 340 grams onion (red, large dice)
- 12 medium mushroom caps
- 355 ml olive oil
- 15 grams garlic crushed
- 1 ½ tsp rosemary dried
- 1/2 tsp thyme dried
- 2 tsp salt
- 1/2 tsp black pepper

Directions:
1. Cut the zucchini and yellow squash into 12 equal slices each.
2. Arrange the vegetables on 12 bamboo skewers. Give each skewer an equal arrangement of vegetable pieces.
3. Place the skewers in a single layer in a hotel pan.
4. Mix the oil, garlic, herbs, salt, and pepper to make a marinade.
5. Pour the marinade over the vegetables, turning them to coat completely.
6. Marinate 1 hour. Turn the skewers once or twice during margination to ensure the vegetables are coated.
7. Remove the skewers from the marinade and let the excess oil drip off.

Vegetable Fritters

Servings| 10   Time| 50 minutes
Nutritional Content (per serving):
Cal| 140   Fat| 6 g   Protein| 4 g   Carbs| 19 g

Ingredients:
- 3 eggs beaten
- 230 ml milk
- 230 grams whole wheat flour
- 1 tbsp baking powder
- ½ tsp salt
- 10 grams honey

Vegetables:
- 340 grams carrot diced, cooked
- 340 grams baby lima beans cooked
- 340 grams asparagus diced, cooked
- 340 grams celery diced, cooked
- 340 grams turnip diccd, cookcd
- 340 grams eggplant diced, cooked
- 340 grams cauliflower diced, cooked
- 340 grams zucchini diced, cooked
- 340 grams parsnips diced, cooked

Directions:
1. Combine the eggs and milk. Mix the flour, baking powder, salt, and honey. Add to the milk and eggs and mix until smooth.
2. Let the batter stand for several hours in a refrigerator. Stir the cold, cooked vegetable into the batter.
3. Drop with a No. 24 scoop into deep fat at 180 °C (350 °F). Toss the content from the scoop carefully in the hot oil. Fry until golden brown.
4. Drain well and serve.

Cucumber Salad

Servings| 4   Time| 10 minutes
Nutritional Content (per serving):
Cal| 98   Fat| 7 g   Protein| 2 g   Carbs| 9 g

Ingredients:

- 2 chopped medium cucumbers peeled and
- 165 grams cherry tomatoes
- ½ red onion thinly sliced
- 2 tbsp red wine vinegar
- 2 tbsp extra-virgin olive oil
- ¼ tsp dried oregano
- ¼ tsp salt
- Freshly ground black pepper

Directions:

1. In a medium bowl, combine the cucumbers, tomatoes, and red onion.
2. In a small bowl, whisk the vinegar, olive oil, oregano, salt, and some pepper. Pour the vinaigrette over the vegetables and toss to coat.
3. Taste and season with more salt and pepper, if desired. Serve immediately or refrigerate in an airtight container for 2 to 3 days.

Quick Coleslaw

Servings| 4   Time| 15 minutes
Nutritional Content (per serving):
Cal| 146   Fat| 13 g   Protein| 2 g   Carbs| 8 g

Ingredients:

- ❖ 60 ml extra-virgin olive oil
- ❖ Juice of 1 lemon
- ❖ 1 garlic clove minced
- ❖ ½ tsp salt
- ❖ 250 grams finely sliced green cabbage

- ❖ 250 grams finely sliced red cabbage
- ❖ 115 grams shredded carrot
- ❖ 4 chopped scallions white and green parts

Directions:

1. In a small bowl, whisk the olive oil, lemon juice, garlic, and salt. Set aside.
2. In a medium bowl, toss together the green and red cabbage, carrot, and scallions.
3. Pour the dressing over the cabbage and mix well to coat. Serve immediately or refrigerate for several hours before serving.

Creamy Tomato Soup

Servings| 4   Time| 30 minutes
Nutritional Content (per serving):
Cal| 103   Fat| 4 g   Protein| 4 g   Carbs| 14 g

Ingredients:

- ❖ 1 tbsp extra-virgin olive oil
- ❖ ½ chopped onion
- ❖ ½ chopped red bell pepper
- ❖ 3 garlic cloves minced
- ❖ 1 can no-salt-added whole tomatoes
- ❖ 375 ml vegetable broth
- ❖ 120 ml skim milk
- ❖ ½ tsp salt
- ❖ ¼ tsp freshly ground black pepper
- ❖ 2 tbsp chopped fresh basil
- ❖ 20 g Parmesan cheese

Directions:

1. In a large pot over medium heat, heat the olive oil.
2. Increase the heat to medium-high and add the onion and red bell pepper. Sauté for 3 to 5 minutes, until softened.
3. Add the garlic, and cook for 30 seconds more, until fragrant.
4. Stir in the tomatoes and their juices and the vegetable broth. Bring to a boil, reduce the heat to maintain a simmer, and cook for 10 minutes.
5. Using an immersion blender, purée the soup in the pot. Alternately, transfer the soup, in batches, to a regular blender, purée the soup, and return it to the pot.
6. Stir in the milk, salt, and pepper. Heat for about 1 minute, until heated through.
7. Stir in the basil and serve, topping each serving with 1 tablespoon of Parmesan (if using).

Creamy Broccoli Soup

Servings| 4   Time| 20 minutes
Nutritional Content (per serving):
Cal| 258   Fat| 12 g   Protein| 12 g   Carbs| 26 g

Ingredients:

- 3 chopped small broccoli crowns
- 500 ml low sodium vegetable broth
- 4 tbsp butter
- 6 tbsp whole-wheat flour
- 710 ml skim milk
- ½ tsp salt
- ¼ tsp freshly ground black pepper

Directions:

1. In a large pot over high heat, combine the broccoli and vegetable broth, and bring to a boil. Reduce the heat to medium, cover the pot, and cook for 7 to 10 minutes, until tender.
2. Meanwhile, in a small saucepan over medium heat, melt the butter. Whisk in the flour and cook for about 1 minute, stirring constantly. While whisking continuously, slowly add the milk until it is all incorporated. Simmer briefly until just thickened.
3. Using an immersion blender, purée the soup in the pot. Alternately, transfer the soup, in batches, to a regular blender, purée the soup, and return it to the pot.
4. Stir the cream sauce into the soup, season with the salt and pepper, and serve.

Sautéed Greens

Servings| 4   Time| 15 minutes
Nutritional Content (per serving):
Cal| 86   Fat| 7 g   Protein| 2 g   Carbs| 5 g

Ingredients:

- ❖ 2 tbsp extra-virgin olive oil
- ❖ 3 garlic cloves minced
- ❖ 450 grams kale
- ❖ Red wine vinegar, for seasoning
- ❖ Salt

Directions:

1. In a large skillet over medium-high heat, heat the olive oil. Add the garlic and cook for 30 seconds, until fragrant.
2. Add the kale to the skillet and stir well. Reduce the heat to medium-low and cover.
3. Cook for 3 to 5 minutes, stirring occasionally, until the greens are tender.
4. Remove the lid, season with vinegar and salt, and serve.

Roasted Beet Salad

Servings| 4   Time| 1 hour 20 minutes
Nutritional Content (per serving):
Cal| 267   Fat| 20 g   Protein| 7g   Carbs| 18 g

Ingredients:

- ❖ 6 medium beets scrubbed tops removed
- ❖ 60 ml balsamic vinegar
- ❖ 60 ml extra-virgin olive oil
- ❖ 1 tsp Dijon mustard
- ❖ Salt
- ❖ Freshly ground black pepper
- ❖ 30 grams walnuts
- ❖ 170 grams baby arugula
- ❖ 60 grams feta cheese

Directions:

1. Set your oven to preheat to 200 °C (400 °F).
2. Using aluminium foil to tightly wrap your beet and arrange on a baking sheet. Roast for 45 to 60 minutes, depending on their size, until tender when pierced with a knife. Remove from the oven, carefully unwrap each beet, and let cool for 10 minutes.
3. Reduce the oven temperature to 180 °C (350 °F).
4. Meanwhile, in a medium bowl, whisk the vinegar, olive oil, and mustard. Season with salt and pepper.
5. On the same baking sheet, spread the walnuts in a single layer. Toast for 5 to 7 minutes, until lightly browned.
6. Using a small knife, peel and slice the beets, and place them in another medium bowl. Add half the vinaigrette and toss to coat.
7. Add the arugula to the remaining vinaigrette and toss to coat.
8. On a serving platter, arrange the arugula and top with the beets. Sprinkle the toasted walnuts and feta cheese over the top and serve.

Cauli-Couscous

Servings| 6   Time| 15 minutes
Nutritional Content (per serving):
Cal| 72   Fat| 0 g   Protein| 3 g   Carbs| 17 g

Ingredients:
- ❖ 1 head cauliflower cored and cut into florets
- ❖ ½ tsp salt
- ❖ ½ tsp ground turmeric
- ❖ 70 grams golden raisins

Directions:
1. In a food processor, pulse the cauliflower several times until it resembles a coarse, couscous-like grain.
2. In a large skillet over medium-high heat, combine the cauliflower, salt, and turmeric. Add just enough water to cover the bottom of the pan. Bring to a simmer, reduce the heat to low, and cover the skillet. Steam for 5 minutes.
3. Remove the lid and cook off any water remaining in the pan. Stir in the raisins and serve.

Quinoa Pilaf

Servings| 6   Time| 45 minutes
Nutritional Content (per serving):
Cal| 196   Fat| 8 g   Protein| 7 g   Carbs| 24 g

Ingredients:

- 60 grams slivered almonds
- 1 tbsp extra-virgin olive oil
- ½ chopped onion
- ½ chopped red bell pepper
- 180 g quinoa
- 60 ml dry white wine
- 310 ml low-sodium vegetable broth
- 1 chopped cucumber peeled and finely
- Zest of 1 lemon
- ½ tsp salt
- ¼ tsp freshly ground black pepper

Directions:

1. Preheat the oven to 180 °C (350 °F).
2. On a baking sheet, spread the almonds in a single layer. Toast for 5 to 7 minutes, until lightly toasted. Set aside.
3. Meanwhile, in a large pan or skillet over medium-high heat, heat the olive oil.
4. Add the onion, and sauté for about 2 minutes, until just starting to soften.
5. Add the red bell pepper, and cook for 5 minutes more, until the vegetables are tender.
6. Add the quinoa to the skillet, and cook for about 2 minutes, stirring constantly, until lightly toasted.
7. Stir in the wine and cook, stirring constantly, until evaporated, about 5 minutes.

8. Add the vegetable broth and bring to a boil. Reduce the heat to maintain a simmer, cover the pan, and cook for 12 to 15 minutes, until all the liquid is evaporated. Turn off the heat and let sit for 10 minutes.
9. Add the cucumber, lemon zest, salt, and pepper, toss well to combine, and serve.

Black Bean and Corn Salad

Servings| 5   Time| 15 minutes
Nutritional Content (per serving):
Cal| 313   Fat| 19 g   Protein| 9 g   Carbs| 32 g

Ingredients:

- ❖ 2 (425 grams) cans reduced-sodium black beans, rinsed and drained
- ❖ 1 red bell pepper, chopped
- ❖ 1 cucumber, chopped
- ❖ 1 avocado, peeled, seeded, and chopped
- ❖ 175 grams fresh, frozen and thawed, or canned and drained corn
- ❖ 160 grams minced red onion
- ❖ 1 jalapeño pepper, seeded and minced
- ❖ 60 grams chopped fresh coriander
- ❖ 60 ml extra-virgin olive oil
- ❖ 3 tablespoons freshly squeezed lime juice
- ❖ 1 teaspoon honey
- ❖ 1 teaspoon ground cumin
- ❖ Salt
- ❖ Freshly ground black pepper

Directions:
1. In a large bowl, stir together the black beans, red bell pepper, cucumber, avocado, corn, red onion, jalapeño, and coriander.
2. 2. In a small bowl, whisk the olive oil, lime juice, honey, and cumin. Season with salt and pepper. Pour the dressing over the salad, mix well to coat, and serve.

Sweet Potato Fries

Servings| 4   Time| 35 minutes
Nutritional Content (per serving):
Cal| 158   Fat| 7 g   Protein| 2 g   Carbs| 23 g

Ingredients:

- ❖ 450 grams sweet potatoes
- ❖ 30 ml extra-virgin olive oil
- ❖ ½ tsp salt

Directions:

1. Preheat the oven to 220 °C (425 °F).
2. In a large bowl, combine the sweet potatoes, olive oil, and salt, and toss to coat.
3. Arrange the sweet potatoes on a baking sheet in a single layer. Bake for about 25 minutes, flipping once or twice during cooking, until the sweet potatoes are tender and crisp, and serve.

Polenta

Servings| 4   Time| 25 minutes
Nutritional Content (per serving):
Cal| 166   Fat| 6 g   Protein| 6 g   Carbs| 24 g

Ingredients:

- 500 ml low-sodium vegetable broth
- 470 ml water
- 1 tsp salt
- 130 grams yellow cornmeal
- 1 tbsp butter
- 20 g shredded Parmesan cheese

Directions:

1. In a medium saucepan over high heat, bring the vegetable broth and water to a boil. Add the salt, and slowly whisk in the cornmeal.
2. Reduce the heat to low and cook for about 15 minutes, stirring regularly, until the polenta thickens and becomes tender.
3. Stir in the butter and Parmesan cheese until melted and serve.

Balsamic Vinaigrette

Servings| 1 cup   Time| 5 minutes
Nutritional Content (per serving):
Cal| 171   Fat| 19 g   Protein| 0 g   Carbs| 2 g

Ingredients:

- ❖ 180 ml extra-virgin olive oil
- ❖ 60 ml balsamic vinegar
- ❖ 2 garlic cloves minced
- ❖ 1 tsp Dijon mustard
- ❖ ½ tsp freshly ground black pepper
- ❖ ¼ tsp salt

Directions:

1. In a small bowl or lidded jar, combine the olive oil, vinegar, garlic, mustard, pepper, and salt.
2. Whisk to combine, or cover and shake until blended. Keep covered and refrigerate for up to 1 month.

Perfect Quinoa Salad

Servings| 6   Time| 30 minutes
Nutritional Content (per serving):
Cal| 200   Fat| 10 g   Protein| 5 g   Carbs| 23 g

Ingredients:

- 180 g quinoa
- 355 ml water
- 1 chopped cucumber finely
- 1 chopped red bell pepper finely
- ½ chopped red onion
- 30 grams fresh flat-leaf parsley
- 60 ml extra-virgin olive oil
- Juice of 2 lemons
- 3 garlic cloves minced
- ½ tsp salt
- ¼ tsp freshly ground black pepper

Directions:

1. In a small saucepan over high heat, combine the quinoa and water. Bring to a boil, reduce the heat to low, cover the pot, and cook for 10 to 15 minutes, until the water is absorbed. Turn off the heat, fluff with a fork, re-cover, and let rest for about 5 minutes.
2. Meanwhile, in a large bowl, toss the cucumber, red bell pepper, red onion, and parsley.
3. In a small bowl, whisk the olive oil, lemon juice, garlic, salt, and pepper. Pour the dressing over the vegetables and toss well to coat. Fold in the quinoa and serve.

Lunch

Roasted Beet Salad with Ricotta Cheese

Servings| 4   Time| 70 minutes
Nutritional Content (per serving):
Cal| 290   Fat| 6 g   Protein| 6 g   Carbs| 12 g

Ingredients:

- ❖ 250 grams red beets large, wrapped in foil
- ❖ 250 grams yellow beets small, wrapped in foil
- ❖ 120 grams mesclun
- ❖ 120 grams mustard vinaigrette
- ❖ 60 grams ricotta cheese
- ❖ 10 grams walnuts chopped

Directions:

1. Bake at 200 °C (400 °F) until the beets are tender, about 1 hour.
2. Cool the beets slightly. Trim the root and stem ends and pull off the peels.
3. Cut the red beets crosswise into thin slices.
4. Cut the yellow beets vertically into quarters.
5. Arrange the sliced red beets in circles on cold salad plates. Toss the mesclun with half the vinaigrette.
6. Drizzle the remaining vinaigrette over the sliced beets.
7. Place a small mound of greens in the centre of each plate.
8. Arrange the quartered yellow beets around the greens.
9. Sprinkle the tops of the salads with the crumbled ricotta and walnuts (if using).

Cioppino (Seafood and Tomato Stew)

Servings| 4   Time| 25 minutes
Nutritional Content (per serving):
Cal| 250   Fat| 8 g   Protein| 23 g   Carbs| 11 g

Ingredients:

- 2 tbsp extra-virgin olive oil
- 1 onion chopped finely
- 1 garlic clove minced
- 110 ml dry white wine
- 400 grams tomato sauce
- 230 grams shrimp peeled and deveined
- 230 grams Cod pin bones removed and cut into 3-cm pieces
- 1 tbsp Italian seasoning
- ½ tsp sea salt
- Pinch red pepper flakes

Directions:
1. Heat the olive oil in a large skillet over medium-high heat until it shimmers.
2. Toss in the onion and cook for 3 minutes, stirring occasionally, or until the onion is translucent.
3. Stir in the garlic and cook for 30 seconds until fragrant.
4. Add the wine and cook for 1 minute, stirring continuously. Stir in the tomato sauce and bring the mixture to a simmer.
5. Add the shrimp and cod, Italian seasoning, salt, and red pepper flakes, and whisk to combine.
6. Continue simmering for about 5 minutes, or until the fish is cooked through.
7. Remove from the heat and serve on plates.

Baked Fish with Tomatoes and Mushrooms

Servings| 4   Time| 30 minutes
Nutritional Content (per serving):
Cal| 350   Fat| 9 g   Protein| 55 g   Carbs| 6 g

Ingredients:

- ❖ 4 fish whole and small 340 grams each
- ❖ Salt to taste
- ❖ Pepper to taste
- ❖ Dried thyme pinch
- ❖ Parsley 4 sprigs
- ❖ Olive oil (as needed)

- ❖ 110 grams onion small dice
- ❖ 30 grams shallots minced
- ❖ 230 grams mushrooms, chopped
- ❖ 180 grams tomato concasse
- ❖ 95 ml dry white wine

Directions:

1. Scale and clean the fish but leaves the heads on. Season the fish inside and out with salt and pepper and put a small pinch of thyme and a sprig of parsley in the cavity of each.
2. Use as many baking pans as possible to hold the fish in a single layer. Oil the pans with a little olive oil.
3. Sauté the onions and shallots in a little olive oil about 1 minute. Add the mushrooms and sauté lightly.
4. Put the sautéed vegetables and the tomatoes in the bottoms of the baking pans. Put the fish in the pans. Oil the tops lightly. Pour in the wine.
5. Bake at 200 °C (400 °F) until the fish is done. The time will vary but will average 15-20 minutes. Base often with the liquid in the pan.
6. Remove the fish and keep them warm until they are plated.
7. Remove the vegetables from the pans with a slotted spoon and check for seasonings. Serve a spoonful of the vegetables with the fish, placing it under or alongside each fish.
8. Strain, degrease, and reduce the cooking liquid slightly. Just before serving, moisten each portion with 1-2 tbsp of the liquid.

Chicken Tortilla Soup

Servings| 4   Time| 45 minutes
Nutritional Content (per serving):
Cal| 191   Fat| 9 g   Protein| 19 g   Carbs| 13 g

Ingredients:
- 1 tbs extra-virgin olive oil
- 1 onion thinly sliced
- 1 garlic clove minced
- Jalapeño pepper diced
- 2 chicken breasts boneless, skinless
- 950 ml chicken broth low-sodium
- 1 roma tomato diced
- ½ teaspoon salt
- 2 corn tortillas cut into thin strips
- Non-stick cooking spray
- Juice of 1 lime
- Minced fresh coriander, for garnish
- 100 grams cheddar cheese shredded, for garnish

Directions:
1. Set your oil to heat up over high heat. Add the onion and cook until fragrant and soft (about 3 to 5 minutes).
2. Add the garlic and jalapeño, and cook until fragrant, about 1 minute more.
3. Add in your salt, tomato, broth, and chicken then leave to come to a boil.
4. Once boiling, switch to medium heat and allow to simmer gently for 20 to 25 minutes or as long as it takes for your chicken breasts to fully cook.
5. Remove the chicken from the pot and set aside. Set your broiler to preheat on high.
6. Lightly coat the tortilla strips with cooking spray then toss. Transfer them onto a baking sheet in a single layer and set to broil for 3 to 5 minutes, flipping once, until crisp.
7. When the chicken is cool enough to handle, shred it with two forks and return to the pot.
8. Season the soup with the lime juice. Serve hot, garnished with coriander, cheese, and tortilla strips.

Goat Cheese and Walnut Salad

Servings| 3   Time| 25 minutes
Nutritional Content (per serving):
Cal| 460   Fat| 40 g   Protein| 17 g   Carbs| 13 g

Ingredients:

- ❖ 50 grams beet
- ❖ 85 grams arugula
- ❖ 60 grams bibb lettuce
- ❖ 260 grams romaine lettuce
- ❖ 90 grams breadcrumbs dry
- ❖ 1/4 tbs dried thyme

- ❖ 1/4 tbs dried basil
- ❖ 1/3 tsp black pepper
- ❖ 180 grams fresh goat's milk cheese preferably in log shape
- ❖ 30 grams walnut pieces
- ❖ Red wine vinaigrette (optional)

Directions:

1. Trim, wash, and dry all the salad greens. Tear the greens into small pieces. Toss well.
2. Mix the herbs, pepper, and crumbs. Slice the cheese into 30 grams pieces.
3. In the seasoned crumbs mix, roll the pieces of cheese to coat them
4. Place the cheese on a sheet pan. Bake at the temperate of 220 °C (425 °F) for 10 minutes.
5. At the same time, toast the walnuts in a dry sauté pan or the oven with the cheese.
6. Toss the greens with the vinaigrette and arrange on cold plates. Top each plate of greens with 2 pieces of cheese and sprinkle with walnuts.

Tomato and Kale Soup

Servings| 4   Time| 25 minutes
Nutritional Content (per serving):
Cal| 170   Fat| 5 g   Protein| 6 g   Carbs| 31 g

Ingredients:
- ❖ 1 tbsp extra-virgin olive oil
- ❖ 1 medium onion chopped
- ❖ 2 carrots finely chopped
- ❖ 3 garlic cloves minced
- ❖ 950 ml vegetable broth, low-sodium
- ❖ 800 grams tomatoes, crushed
- ❖ ½ tsp dried oregano
- ❖ ¼ tsp dried basil
- ❖ 800 grams baby kale leaves, chopped
- ❖ ¼ tsp Salt

Directions:
1. Over medium heat, set a large pot on with your oil. Add in your carrots and onions.
2. Sauté for 3 to 5 minutes until they begin to soften. Add the garlic and sauté for 30 seconds more, until fragrant.
3. Add the basil, oregano, tomato, and vegetable broth then leave to boil. Reduce the heat to low and simmer for 5 minutes.
4. Using an immersion blender, purée the soup. Add the kale and simmer for 3 more minutes.
5. Season with the salt. Serve immediately.

Panko Coconut Shrimp

Servings| 4   Time| 20 minutes
Nutritional Content (per serving):
Cal| 181   Fat| 4 g   Protein| 29 g   Carbs| 9 g

Ingredients:
- 2 egg whites
- 1 tbsp water
- 110 grams whole-wheat panko breadcrumbs
- 70 grams coconut flakes unsweetened
- ½ tsp turmeric
- ½ tsp ground coriander
- ½ tsp ground cumin
- salt
- 450 grams raw shrimp large, peeled, deveined, and patted dry
- Non-stick cooking spray

Directions:
1. Preheat the air fry to 200 °C (400 °F). In a shallow dish, beat the egg whites and water until slightly foamy. Set aside.
2. In a separate shallow dish, mix the breadcrumbs, coconut flakes, turmeric, coriander, cumin, and salt, and stir until well combined.
3. Dredge the shrimp in the egg mixture, shaking off any excess, then coat them in the crumb-coconut mixture.
4. Spritz the air fryer basket with non-stick cooking spray and arrange the coated shrimp in the basket.
5. Air fry for 6 to 8 minutes, flipping the shrimp once during cooking, or until the shrimp are golden brown and cooked through.
6. Let the shrimp cool for 5 minutes before serving.

Grilled Spiced Turkey Burger

Servings| 3   Time| 35 minutes
Nutritional Content (per serving):
Cal| 250   Fat| 14 g   Protein| 27 g   Carbs| 2 g

Ingredients:

- 50 grams onion chopped fine
- 1/3 tbsp extra virgin olive oil
- 300 grams turkey ground
- 1/3 tbsp salt
- 1/3 tbsp curry powder
- 2/5 tsp lemon zest grated
- 1/8 tsp pepper
- 1/8 tsp cinnamon
- 1/4 tsp coriander ground
- 1/8 tsp cumin ground
- 1/8 tsp Cardamom ground
- 50 ml water
- Tomato Raisin Chutney (as desired)
- Coriander leaves (as desired)

Directions:
1. Cook the onions in the oil until soft. Cool completely.
2. Combine the turkey, onions, spices, water, and salt in a bowl. Toss until mixed.
3. Divide the mixture into portions (as desired). Form each portion into a thick patty.
4. Broil or grill until well done, but do not overcook it, or the burger will dry.
5. Plate the burgers. Place a spoonful of chutney on top of each burger or place it on the side with a small number of greens.
6. You can serve the burger and garnish as a sandwich on whole-grain bread.

Tomato Tea Party Sandwiches

Servings| 4   Time| 15 minutes
Nutritional Content (per serving):
Cal| 230   Fat| 16 g   Protein| 6 g   Carbs| 19 g

Ingredients:

- 4 slices whole wheat bread
- 4 1/3 tbsp extra virgin olive oil
- 2 1/8 tbsp basil minced
- 4 thick tomato slices
- 110 grams ricotta cheese
- Dash of pepper

Directions:
1. Toast bread to your preference. Spread 2 tsp. olive oil on each slice of bread. Add the cheese.
2. Top with tomato, then sprinkle with basil and pepper. Serve with lemon water.

Curried Carrot Soup

Servings| 6   Time| 15 minutes

Nutritional Content (per serving):

Cal| 145   Fat| 11 g   Protein| 2 g   Carbs| 13 g

Ingredients:

- 1 tbsp extra-virgin olive oil
- 1 onion coarsely chopped
- 2 celery stalks chopped
- 1½ tsp curry powder
- 1 tsp ground cumin
- 1 tsp fresh ginger minced
- 6 Carrots roughly chopped
- 950 ml vegetable broth low-sodium
- Salt
- 1 can coconut milk
- ¼ tsp Ground black pepper
- 1 tbsp fresh cilantro chopped

Directions:

1. Heat an Instant Pot to high and add the olive oil. Sauté the onion and celery for 2 to 3 minutes.
2. Add the curry powder, cumin, and ginger to the pot and cook until fragrant, about 30 seconds.
3. Add the carrots, vegetable broth, and salt to the pot.
4. Close and seal and set for 5 minutes on high. Allow the pressure to release naturally.
5. In a blender jar, carefully purée the soup in batches and transfer back to the pot.
6. Stir in the coconut milk and pepper, and heat through. Top with the cilantro and serve.

Tuna, Hummus, and Veggie Wraps

Servings| 2   Time| 2 minutes

Nutritional Content (per serving):

Cal| 191   Fat| 5 g   Protein| 26 g   Carbs| 5 g

Ingredients:

For the hummus:

- ❖ 240 grams chickpeas canned low sodium drained and rinsed
- ❖ 1 garlic clove
- ❖ 2 tbsp tahini
- ❖ 1 tbsp extra-virgin olive oil
- ❖ Juice of ½ lemon
- ❖ Salt
- ❖ 2 tbsp Water

For the wraps:

- ❖ 1 can chunk light tuna in water, drained
- ❖ 4 large lettuce leaves
- ❖ 1 red bell pepper seeded and cut into strips
- ❖ 1 cucumber

Directions:

To make the hummus:

1. In a blender jar, combine the chickpeas, tahini, olive oil, garlic, lemon juice, salt, and water.
2. Process until smooth. Taste and adjust with additional lemon juice or salt, as needed.

To make the wraps:

1. On each lettuce leaf, spread 1 tablespoon of hummus, and divide the tuna among the leaves.
2. Top each with several strips of red pepper and cucumber slices.
3. Roll up the lettuce leaves, folding in the two shorter sides and rolling away from you, like a burrito. Serve.

Salmon Milano

Servings| 6   Time| 30 minutes
Nutritional Content (per serving):
Cal| 445   Fat| 24 g   Protein| 55 g   Carbs| 2 g

Ingredients:
- 1.1 kg salmon filet
- 2 tomatoes sliced
- 110 grams margarine
- 150 grams basil pesto

Directions:
1. Heat the oven to 200 °C (400 °F). Line a baking sheet with foil, making sure it covers the sides.
2. Place another large piece of foil onto the baking sheet and place the salmon filet on top of it.
3. Place the pesto and margarine in blender or food processor and pulse until smooth. Spread evenly over salmon. Place tomato slices on top.
4. Wrap the foil around the salmon, tenting around the top to prevent foil from touching the salmon as much as possible.
5. Bake 15 to 25 minutes, or salmon flakes easily with a fork. Serve.

Veggie Shish Kebabs

Servings| 3   Time| 10 minutes
Nutritional Content (per serving):
Cal| 350   Fat| 6 g   Protein| 15 g   Carbs| 61 g

Ingredients:
- 9 skewers wooden
- 9 cherry tomatoes
- 9 mozzarella balls
- Basil leaves
- 1 tsp olive oil
- Zucchini 3 sliced
- Dash of pepper

For Serving:
- 6 slices whole wheat bread

Directions:
1. Stab 1 cherry tomato, low-fat mozzarella ball, zucchini, and basil leaf onto each skewer.
2. Place skewers on a plate and drizzle with olive oil. Finish with a sprinkle of pepper.
3. Set your bread to toast. Serve 2 bread slices with 3 kebobs.
4. Enjoy!

Crispy Falafel

Servings| 3   Time| 30 minutes
Nutritional Content (per serving):
Cal| 328   Fat| 11 g   Protein| 48 g   Carbs| 48 g

Ingredients:

- ❖ 240 grams chickpeas drained and rinsed
- ❖ 90 grams parsley chopped with stems removed
- ❖ 70 grams coriander chopped with stems removed
- ❖ 70 grams dill chopped with stems removed
- ❖ 4 cloves garlic minced
- ❖ 1 tbsp sesame seeds toasted
- ❖ ½ tbsp coriander
- ❖ ½ tbsp black pepper
- ❖ ½ tbsp cumin
- ❖ ½ tbsp baking powder
- ❖ ½ tbsp cayenne
- ❖ Olive oil for frying

Directions:

1. Thoroughly dry your chickpeas with a paper towel.
2. Place the parsley, coriander, and dill in a food processor and pulse until it forms mulch.
3. Add in the chickpeas, garlic, coriander, black pepper, cumin, baking powder, and cayenne. Pulse this mixture until smooth and well combined.
4. Transfer the mixture to an airtight container and let it sit in the fridge for about an hour, or until stiff.
5. Remove the mixture from the refrigerator and stir in the baking powder and sesame seeds until well combined.
6. Scoop the mixture into a pan with 8 cm of olive oil over medium heat to create patties.
7. Keep in mind as you create the patties that you are aiming to make 12 with the mixture.
8. Let the falafel patties fry for 1-2 minutes on each side or until golden brown.
9. Once your falafel patties are nicely browned, transfer them to a plate lined with paper towels to finish crisping.
10. Dip, dunk, fill, and enjoy!

Margherita Pizza

Servings|6   Time|35 minutes
Nutritional Content (per serving):
Cal| 426   Fat| 13 g   Protein| 21 g   Carbs| 60 g

Ingredients:

For The Dough:

- ❖ 235 ml warm water
- ❖ 1 tsp sugar
- ❖ 2¼ tsp active dry yeast
- ❖ 180 grams whole-wheat flour
- ❖ 180 grams all-purpose flour
- ❖ 2 tbsp extra-virgin olive oil
- ❖ 1 tsp salt

For The Pizza:

- ❖ Extra - virgin olive oil, for preparing the baking sheet
- ❖ 1 can no-salt-added diced tomatoes drained
- ❖ 230 grams mozzarella cheese
- ❖ 5 grams fresh basil leaves

Directions:

To Make the Dough:

1. In a stand mixer fitted with a dough hook, combine the warm water, sugar, and yeast. Mix well and let sit for about 5 minutes, until bubbly.
2. Add the whole-wheat and all-purpose flours, 1 tablespoon of olive oil, and the salt. Mix on low speed until the dough comes together.
3. Increase the speed to medium and continue mixing for about 5 minutes, until the dough becomes elastic and shiny.
4. Coat a bowl larger than your dough with the remaining 1 tablespoon of olive oil and transfer the dough to the bowl.
5. Use plastic wrap to cover the bowl, set it in a warm place, and let rise until doubled in size, about 1 hour.
6. Punch the dough down and form it into a ball. Let rest for 15 minutes.

To Make the Pizza

7. Preheat the oven to 260°C (500 °F). Lightly coat a baking sheet with olive oil. In a blender, process the tomatoes until puréed.
8. Place the dough ball on the prepared baking sheet and use your hands to stretch and shape it to the size of the baking sheet.
9. Spread the tomato sauce on the pizza dough. Cover with the mozzarella slices, and top with the basil leaves.
10. Bake for 12 to 18 minutes, until the cheese is melted, and the crust is browned in spots.
11. Remove from the oven and let cool for 5 minutes. Cut into 6 slices and serve.

Chickpea, Tomato, and Kale Soup

Servings|4   Time| 25 minutes
Nutritional Content (per serving):
Cal| 273   Fat| 6 g   Protein| 13 g   Carbs| 42 g

Ingredients:

- ❖ 1 tbsp extra-virgin olive oil
- ❖ 1 chopped onion
- ❖ 3 garlic cloves minced
- ❖ 1 (439g) can chickpeas drained
- ❖ 1 (425) can no-salt-added diced tomatoes
- ❖ 1L low-sodium vegetable broth
- ❖ 270 grams finely chopped kale leaves
- ❖ ½ tsp salt
- ❖ Freshly ground black pepper
- ❖ 25 grams Parmesan cheese

Directions:

1. In a large pot over medium-high heat, heat the olive oil. Add the onion, and sauté for 3 to 5 minutes, until softened.
2. Add the garlic, and cook for 30 seconds, until fragrant. Stir in the chickpeas and tomatoes and their juices. Add the vegetable broth and bring to a boil.
3. Reduce the heat to low, add the kale, and simmer for 2 to 3 minutes, until the kale wilts. Season with the salt and some pepper.
4. Serve topped with the Parmesan.

Falafel Sandwich

Servings| 6   Time| 30 minutes
Nutritional Content (per serving):
Cal| 356   Fat| 8 g   Protein| 13 g   Carbs| 61 g

Ingredients:

- ❖ 2 (425 g cans) chickpeas drained
- ❖ 1 chopped medium onion roughly
- ❖ 5 garlic cloves minced divided
- ❖ 15 grams packed fresh parsley leaves
- ❖ Juice of 1 lemon
- ❖ 2 tbsp extra-virgin olive oil
- ❖ 1 tsp ground cumin
- ❖ 1 tsp ground coriander
- ❖ 1¼ tsp salt
- ❖ 2 tsp baking powder
- ❖ 110 grams plain non-fat Greek yogurt
- ❖ 3 whole-wheat pita pockets halved
- ❖ Sliced cucumbers, for serving
- ❖ Sliced tomatoes, for serving

Directions:

1. In a food processor, combine the chickpeas, onion, 3 garlic cloves, parsley, lemon juice, 1 tablespoon of olive oil, cumin, coriander, and 1 teaspoon of salt.
2. Pulse several times, until the chickpeas and onions are chopped coarsely and mixed but not puréed.
3. Add the baking powder and pulse several more times, until it is mixed in and the mixture forms into a ball. Form the mixture into 12 small balls and press the balls into patties.
4. In a small bowl, whisk the yogurt with the remaining ¼ teaspoon of salt and 2 garlic cloves. Set aside.
5. In a large skillet over medium heat, heat the remaining 1 tablespoon of olive oil.

6. Working in batches, cook the patties for 2 to 3 minutes per side, gently flipping once during cooking, until browned and crisp.
7. To serve, place two patties into a half pita, top with cucumber and tomato slices, and garnish with a spoonful of yogurt.

Butternut Squash and Mushroom Lasagne

Servings| 8   Time| 1 hour 15 minutes
Nutritional Content (per serving):
Cal| 352   Fat| 15 g   Protein| 26 g   Carbs| 30 g

Ingredients:

- ❖ 1 butternut squash
- ❖ 2 tbsp butter
- ❖ 1 chopped onion
- ❖ 220 grams chopped brown mushrooms
- ❖ Salt
- ❖ Freshly ground black pepper
- ❖ 425 grams low-fat ricotta cheese
- ❖ 425 grams low-fat cottage cheese

- ❖ 2 large eggs
- ❖ 3 tbsp chopped fresh thyme
- ❖ 3 tbsp chopped fresh sage
- ❖ 170 grams grated mozzarella cheese
- ❖ 50 grams grated Parmesan cheese
- ❖ 1 package no-boil lasagne noodles

Directions:

1. Poke the squash several times with a fork. Microwave it at high power for 6 to 8 minutes, depending on your microwave, until tender. Set aside and let cool.
2. Preheat the oven to 180 °C (350 °F). Meanwhile, in a large skillet over medium-high heat, melt the butter.
3. Add the onion, and cook for 3 to 5 minutes, until just starting to soften. Add the mushrooms, and cook until the liquid evaporates, about 5 minutes.
4. Season lightly with salt and pepper. In a large bowl, stir together the ricotta, cottage cheese, eggs, and 1½ tablespoons each of thyme and sage until well mixed.

5. Using a vegetable peeler or sharp knife, peel the squash and chop into 1 pieces. Transfer to another large bowl, and gently toss with the remaining 1½ tablespoons each of sage and thyme.
6. Spread about 200 g of the ricotta cheese mixture on the bottom of a 23-by-33-cm baking dish.
7. Arrange 3 noodles on top of the cheese. On the noodles, spread about 200 g of the ricotta mixture, 210 g of squash, 60 g of mushrooms, and 85 g of mozzarella cheese.
8. Add 3 more noodles and repeat the same process for another layer.
9. Top with the remaining 3 noodles, the remaining 200 g of ricotta mixture, and the remaining 85 g of mozzarella.
10. Sprinkle the top with the grated Parmesan cheese. Cover the dish with aluminium foil and bake for 40 minutes, until the noodles are softened, and the Lasagne is bubbly.
11. Remove the foil and bake for 5 minutes more, until the top is golden brown. Let stand for 10 minutes before serving.

Spaghetti with Chickpea and Mushroom Marinara

Servings| 4   Time| 40 minutes
Nutritional Content (per serving):
Cal| 456   Fat| 6 g   Protein| 18 g   Carbs| 88 g

Ingredients:

- ❖ 425 grams low-sodium chickpeas rinsed and drained
- ❖ 1 tbsp extra-virgin olive oil
- ❖ 220 grams fresh mushrooms
- ❖ 1 chopped onion finely
- ❖ 3 garlic cloves minced
- ❖ 800 grams no-salt-added whole tomatoes
- ❖ 1 tbsp honey
- ❖ ½ tsp salt
- ❖ ¼ tsp red pepper flakes
- ❖ black pepper
- ❖ 225 grams whole-wheat spaghetti

Directions:

1. In a food processer, pulse the chickpeas several times until coarsely ground. In a large skillet over medium-high heat, heat the olive oil.
2. Add the mushrooms and onion, and cook for 5 to 7 minutes, until softened and the liquid has evaporated.
3. Add the garlic, and cook for 30 seconds, until fragrant.
4. Use your hand or a spoon to break apart the tomatoes in the can. Add the tomatoes and their juices to the skillet, along with the honey, salt, red pepper flakes, and black pepper.
5. Add the chickpeas to the skillet. Bring to a boil, reduce the heat to medium-low, and simmer for 10 minutes.
6. Meanwhile, fill a large pot halfway with water and bring to a boil over high heat. Cook the pasta according to the package directions, until al dente. Drain.
7. Serve the pasta topped with the marinara sauce.

Simple Salmon Burgers

Servings| 4   Time| 20 minutes
Nutritional Content (per serving):
Cal| 321   Fat| 16 g   Protein| 22 g   Carbs| 23 g

Ingredients:

- 2 (170 grams cans) salmon
- 1 large egg
- 22 grams whole-wheat breadcrumbs
- 2 garlic cloves minced
- Juice of 1 lemon
- 1 tbsp whole-grain or Dijon mustard
- ¼ tsp salt
- ¼ tsp freshly ground black pepper
- 1 tbsp extra-virgin olive oil
- 4 hamburger buns, whole-wheat
- Lettuce, for serving
- Sliced tomato, for serving
- Mayonnaise, for serving

Directions:

1. Stir together the salmon, salt, egg, breadcrumbs, garlic, lemon juice, pepper, and mustard. Form the mixture into 4 patties.
2. In a large skillet over medium-high heat, heat the olive oil.
3. Add the patties and cook for 4 to 5 minutes per side, until golden brown.
4. Serve on the buns, topped with lettuce, tomato, and mayonnaise.

Salmon and Veggie Bake

Servings| 4   Time| 37 minutes
Nutritional Content (per serving):
Cal| 247   Fat| 14 g   Protein| 24 g   Carbs| 8 g

Ingredients:

- ❖ 1 medium zucchini, chopped into 1-inch pieces
- ❖ Juice of 1 lemon
- ❖ 1 red bell pepper, chopped into 1-inch pieces
- ❖ 1 medium onion, cut into wedges
- ❖ 2 tablespoons olive oil, extra-virgin, divided

- ❖ ½ teaspoon salt, divided
- ❖ ½ teaspoon black pepper, divided
- ❖ 3 garlic cloves, minced
- ❖ 2 tsp Dijon mustard
- ❖ 1 pound salmon fillet, cut into 4 pieces

Directions:

1. Set the oven to preheat to 220 °C (425 °F). Combine the zucchini, red bell pepper, and onion. Add 1 tablespoon of olive oil and toss to coat.
2. Season with ¼ teaspoon each of salt and pepper. Spread the vegetables on a baking sheet in a single layer and bake for 10 minutes.
3. Whisk the remaining tablespoon of olive oil with the garlic, mustard, lemon juice, and remaining ¼ teaspoon each of salt and pepper. Divide the mixture among the salmon fillets and rub it into the flesh.
4. Once the vegetables have cooked for 10 minutes, nestle the salmon fillets on top of them.
5. Bake for 10 to 12 minutes more, until the salmon flakes easily with a fork and the vegetables are tender. Serve the salmon with the vegetables.

Baked Parmesan-Crusted Halibut

Servings| 4   Time| 25 minutes
Nutritional Content (per serving):
Cal| 194   Fat| 8 g   Protein| 26 g   Carbs| 5 g

Ingredients:

- ❖ Non - stick cooking spray
- ❖ 25 grams whole-wheat panko breadcrumbs
- ❖ 25 grams shredded Parmesan cheese
- ❖ 1 tbsp minced fresh parsley leaves
- ❖ ½ tsp garlic powder
- ❖ ½ tsp salt
- ❖ ¼ tsp freshly ground black pepper
- ❖ Juice of ½ lemon
- ❖ 1 tbsp extra-virgin olive oil
- ❖ 455 grams halibut fillet

Directions:

1. Preheat the oven to 230 °C (450 °F). Place a rack on a baking sheet, and lightly spray with cooking spray.
2. On a large plate, combine the panko, Parmesan, parsley, garlic powder, salt, and pepper, and mix well.
3. Pour the lemon juice and olive oil over both sides of the halibut and press the halibut into the coating mixture. Flip the fish and press the coating onto the other side.
4. Transfer the fish to the prepared rack on the baking sheet, and lightly spray the top of the fish with cooking spray. Bake for 12 to 15 minutes, until the fish flakes easily with a fork, and serve.

Herb- Roasted Chicken Breast

Servings|4-6   Time| 30 minutes
Nutritional Content (per serving):
Cal|153   Fat| 5 g   Protein| 26 g   Carbs| 1 g

Ingredients:

- ❖ 1 tablespoon extra-virgin olive oil
- ❖ ½ teaspoon dried oregano
- ❖ 1 teaspoon chopped fresh thyme
- ❖ ½ teaspoon garlic powder
- ❖ ½ teaspoon onion powder
- ❖ 4 boneless skinless chicken breasts
- ❖ ½ teaspoon salt

Directions:
1. Preheat the oven to 200 °C (400 °F).
2. In a small bowl, stir together the olive oil, oregano, thyme, garlic powder, onion powder, and salt.
3. Place the chicken breasts on a baking sheet or in a baking dish and rub both sides with the herb mixture. Leave a couple of inches between each breast.
4. Bake for 20 to 25 minutes, until the juices run clear and the internal temperature measures 70 °C (160 °F) on an instant-read thermometer.
5. Let the chicken rest for 5 minutes before slicing and serving.

Turkey Meat Loaf

Servings| 6   Time| 1 hour 15 minutes
Nutritional Content (per serving):
Cal| 187   Fat| 6 g   Protein| 28 g   Carbs| 7 g

Ingredients:

- ❖ Non-stick cooking spray
- ❖ 1 tbsp extra-virgin olive oil
- ❖ 1 chopped onion
- ❖ 3 garlic cloves minced
- ❖ 680 grams ground turkey
- ❖ 20 grams whole-wheat breadcrumbs
- ❖ 1 large egg
- ❖ 1 tsp salt
- ❖ ½ tsp freshly ground black pepper
- ❖ 55 grams ketchup

Directions:

1. Preheat the oven to 180 °C (350 °F). Lightly coat an 20-by-10-cm loaf pan with cooking spray. Set aside.
2. In a small skillet over medium heat, heat the olive oil. Add the onion and garlic, and sauté for 3 to 5 minutes, until the onion is softened. Remove from the heat, transfer to a large bowl, and let cool for about 5 minutes.
3. Once cooled, add the ground turkey, breadcrumbs, egg, salt, and pepper. Mix well to combine.
4. Press the mixture into the prepared loaf pan and spread the ketchup over the top of the loaf.
5. Bake for 50 to 55 minutes, until the internal temperature measures 70°C (160 °F) on an instant-read thermometer.
6. Remove from the oven and let stand for about 10 minutes before slicing into 6 pieces and serving.

Dinner

Ras-El-Hanout Chicken Traybake

Servings| 4   Time| 70 minutes
Nutritional Content (per serving):
Cal| 360   Fat|6 g   Protein| 45 g   Carbs| 30 g

Ingredients:

- 170 grams chicken breast fillets
- 400 grams sweet potatoes, peeled and cubed
- 2 garlic cloves
- 400 grams carrots peeled and cubed
- 1 tbsp olive oil
- 1 sprigs thyme handful

- Red onion large, sliced in wedges
- 2 tsp ras-el-hanout spice mix
- 2 tsp lemon quartered
- 2 tsp coriander handful, finely chopped
- Salt and black pepper
- 4 tbsp yoghurt low-fat natural, to serve

Directions:

5. Set the oven temperature to 90 °C (195 °F). In a roasting pan, combine the carrots and sweet potatoes. Season with salt and pepper and drizzle with oil.
6. Let it roast for 10 minutes. Stir in the onion and garlic. Continue to roast for 20 more minutes.
7. Cook the chicken breasts in a roasting pan with the lemon quarters in a single layer. Add ras-el-hanout, thyme, and olive oil to everything.
8. The chicken should be cooked through after another 15-20 minutes of roasting. Add the coriander and stir well.
9. Slice the lemon and divide chicken between four plates. Squeeze lemon juice over each and serve with yoghurt.

Light Lemony Pasta and Spinach Bake

Servings| 4   Time| 15 minutes
Nutritional Content (per serving):
Cal| 450   Fat| 11 g   Protein| 24 g   Carbs| 63 g

Ingredients:
- 2 tsp olive oil
- 300 grams macaroni dried
- 1 garlic clove sliced thinly
- 200 grams broccoli, florets
- 1 spring onions thinly sliced
- 100 grams baby spinach, leaves
- 1 tbsp flour plain
- 2 bay leaves
- 300 ml skimmed milk
- Zest of 1 lemon
- 1 tsp wholegrain mustard
- Salt and black pepper
- 100 grams parmesan cheese, finely grated

Salad:
- 1 tsp olive oil
- Lemon juice, a squeeze
- Mixed salad

Directions:
1. Prepare the oven by preheating it to 200 °C (400 °F). Cook the macaroni for 6 minutes in boiling water.
2. Stir in your broccoli then cook for another two minutes. Switch off the heat, add in your spinach then allow to stand covered for another 2 minutes. Drain then set aside
3. Set your oil to get hot in a heavy-set frying pan. Add in your spring onions and cook until fragrant (2 minutes). Next, stir in your garlic the garlic and continue to stir while cooking for 2 more minutes.
4. Stir in your flour and cook until incorporated (about 2 minutes). Pour in your milk in a slow stream, season then add in your bay leaves.
5. Allow to simmer until thickened (about 2-3 minutes). Discard your bay leaves.
6. Stir in your lemon zest, ¾ of your parmesan and mustard, then season to taste.
7. Transfer your broccoli and pasta to a shallow baking dish. Top with your sauce and mix to combine.
8. Add the rest of your cheese evenly on top of your pasta and broccoli then set to bake until beautifully melted (about 15-20 minutes).
9. Serve with your salad. Enjoy!

Butter-Lemon Grilled Cod on Asparagus

Servings| 4   Time| 20 minutes
Nutritional Content (per serving):
Cal| 158   Fat| 6 g   Protein| 23 g   Carbs| 6 g

Ingredients:
- 450 grams asparagus spears, ends trimmed
- Cooking spray
- 4 cod fillets (110g), rinsed and patted dry
- Black pepper optional
- 60 grams light butter with canola oil
- Juice and zest of 1 medium lemon
- Salt optional

Directions:
1. Heat a grill pan over medium-high heat.
2. Spray the asparagus spears with cooking spray. Cook the asparagus for 6 to 8 minutes until fork-tender, flipping occasionally.
3. Transfer to a large platter and keep warm.
4. Spray both sides of fillets with cooking spray. Season with ¼ teaspoon black pepper, if needed.
5. Add the fillets to the pan and sear each side for 3 minutes until opaque.
6. Meantime, in a small bowl, whisk together the light butter, lemon zest, and ¼ teaspoon salt (if desired).
7. Spoon and spread the mixture all over the asparagus. Place the fish on top and squeeze the lemon juice over the fish.
8. Serve immediately.

Mediterranean Sushi

Servings| 4   Time| 15 minutes
Nutritional Content (per serving):
Cal| 408   Fat| 20 g   Protein| 36 g   Carbs| 24 g

Ingredients:
- ❖ 12 large cucumbers
- ❖ 250 grams tomatoes (sun-dried, diced)
- ❖ 550 grams hummus
- ❖ 400 grams feta cheese (low-fat, crumbled)
- ❖ 24 cloves garlic (minced)
- ❖ Dash pepper

Directions:
1. Using a vegetable sheer, peel the outside skin off the cucumber. Create 6 thin pieces by slicing lengthwise.
2. Lay cucumber slices out side-by-side on a cutting board. Layer about 1 ½ teaspoon of hummus over each cucumber slice.
3. Top each slice with 1 ½ teaspoon sun-dried tomatoes and low-fat feta cheese. Sprinkle with pepper.
4. Pick up the end of a cucumber slice that is closest to you and begin to roll so that ingredients are on the inside.
5. Ensure not to roll too tight or the filling will squish out. Secure each roll with a toothpick.
6. Repeat steps 8-9 for the remaining slices of cucumber. Plate and enjoy it!

Pan- Smoked Trout Fillet with Pepper Salad

Servings| 3   Time| 20 minutes
Nutritional Content (per serving):
Cal| 370   Fat| 25 g   Protein| 29 g   Carbs| 9 g

Ingredients:
- 300 grams trout fillet
- 2 tbsp extra virgin olive oil
- 1/4 tsp ground coriander
- 1/4 tsp ground cumin
- 1/8 tsp ground cloves
- 1/4 tsp ground fennel
- 1/4 tsp black pepper
- 1/4 tsp Salt
- 340 grams roasted pepper salad

Directions:
1. Cut the trout fillets into portions. Brush the trout lightly with oil.
2. Sprinkle your spices and salt lightly on top of your fish in an even layer.
3. Set up a smoke roasting system. Set your sawdust or wood chips to get hot in a pan on the stove until it begins to smoke.
4. Lay the trout fillets on the rack, cover, and turn the heat to medium-low. Set to smoke for about 2 minutes.
5. Remove from smoke and set to bake in a preheated 200 °C (400 °F) oven. Roast until the fish is fully cooked through (about 8-10 minutes).
6. Serves immediately with pepper salad.

Pan-Smoked Spiced Chicken Breasts with Fruit Salsa

Servings| 3   Time| 35 minutes
Nutritional Content (per serving):
Cal| 200   Fat| 6 g   Protein| 7 g   Carbs| 29 g

Ingredients:
- 1/2 tbsp paprika
- 1/2 tbsp ground cumin
- 1/4 tsp dried thyme
- ½ tsp ground coriander
- ½ tsp salt
- 1/4 tsp pepper
- 3 chicken breasts boneless and skinless, 140 grams each
- Extra virgin olive oil (as needed)
- 280 grams wheatberries with pecans and poblanos
- 170 grams fruit salsa
- Coriander sprigs (as needed, for garnish, optional)

Directions:
1. Combine the cumin, paprika, thyme, salt, pepper, and coriander. Coat the breast with the spice mixture.
2. Brush with oil lightly. Allow marinating, refrigerated, 3-4 hours.
3. Set up a smoke-roasting system. Heat the pan of sawdust or wood chips on the stovetop until smoke appears.
4. Place the chicken on a rack and cover it. Turn the heat to medium. Smoke roast 10 minutes.
5. Transfer the pan to an oven preheated to 200 °C (400 °F) and roast for another 10 minutes.
6. For each portion, place an 85 g portion of wheatberries on the centre of a plate.
7. Slice a chicken breast on the diagonal and arrange the slices, overlapping, on top of the wheatberries.
8. Spoon 55 g salsa next to the chicken and wheatberries. Garnish with coriander.

Baked Chicken with Brown Rice & Veggies

Servings| 3   Time| 70 minutes
Nutritional Content (per serving):
Cal| 532   Fat| 31 g   Protein| 40 g   Carbs| 23 g

Ingredients:

- 30 grams whole wheat flour
- 1½ tsp salt
- 1/8 tsp white pepper
- 1/4 tsp paprika
- 1/8 tsp dried thyme
- 3 roma tomato large, sliced
- 85 grams broccoli cut in florets
- 1 bunch parsley stems removed
- 850 grams fryer chicken parts
- 85g extra virgin olive oil
- 230 grams brown rice
- 480 ml water

Directions:

1. Combine the flour and seasonings in a pan. Dry the chicken pieces with paper towels if they are wet. Dredge in the seasoned flour.
2. Place the chicken in the Extra Virgin Olive Oil so that it is coated fully. Let excess drip off.
3. Place the chicken on a sheet pan, with the skin side up. If using both dark and light meat parts, place them on separate pans. Add your broccoli in around your chicken.
4. Bake the chicken at 200 °C (400 °F) until done, about 45 mins.
5. Rinse your brown rice and set it on high heat with your ½ tsp salt and water. Cover and allow to come to a boil.
6. Switch to a low heat to simmer for another 45 minutes. Switch off your heat and leave covered for about 10 minutes.
7. When ready to serve. Split your rice, chicken, and tomatoes evenly and store or enjoy.

Fresh Rosemary Trout

Servings| 2   Time| 15 minutes
Nutritional Content (per serving):
Cal| 180   Fat| 9 g   Protein| 24 g   Carbs| 0 g

Ingredients:
- ❖ 4 to 6 fresh rosemary sprigs
- ❖ 220 grams trout fillets (rinsed and patted dry)
- ❖ ½ tsp olive oil
- ❖ ⅛ tsp salt
- ❖ ⅛ tsp pepper
- ❖ 1 tsp fresh lemon juice

Directions:
1. Preheat the oven to 180 °C (350 °F).
2. Put the rosemary sprigs in a small baking pan in a single row. Spread the fillets on the top of the rosemary sprigs.
3. Brush both sides of each piece of fish with the olive oil. Sprinkle with the salt, pepper, and lemon juice.
4. Bake in the preheated oven for 7 to 8 minutes, or until the fish is opaque and flakes easily.
5. Divide the fillets between two plates and serve hot.

Tomato Basil Stuffed Peppers

Servings| 6   Time| 85 minutes
Nutritional Content (per serving):
Cal| 350   Fat| 13 g   Protein| 14 g   Carbs| 46 g

Ingredients:

- 450 grams tofu (crumbled)
- 4 bell peppers
- 1 can tomato sauce
- 350 grams brown rice cooked
- 80 ml heavy cream
- 70 grams basil (chopped)

- 170 grams feta cheese
- 3 garlic cloves (minced)
- ½ onion (diced)
- 1 tbsp olive oil
- Dash of pepper

Directions:
1. Preheat oven to 200 ºC (400 ºF).
2. Slice the tops off the peppers and scoop out their insides. Discard them and set the peppers aside.
3. Put the tofu in a bowl and fold the pepper into it until evenly distributed.
4. Place the pan with the olive oil over medium heat.
5. When the oil is hot, add the onion and let it cook for about 5 minutes or until translucent.
6. Once the onion is translucent, add 2 garlic cloves and cook for 1 minute or until fragrant.
7. As soon as the garlic is fragrant, add the seasoned the crumbled tofu and let it cook for 10-15 minutes or until cooked through.
8. While the tofu cooks, combine the heavy cream, and the left-over garlic clove and mix.
9. Transfer this mixture to a saucepan. Place the saucepan on low heat and stir in some basil, leaving a little bit to garnish your peppers later.
10. Stir the brown rice and feta cheese into the tofu mixture until well combined.
11. Pour half of the tomato sauce mixture into the pan and stir again until well combined. Remove from heat.
12. Line your bell peppers close together and divide the frying pan mixture between them, pouring it into each pepper until full.
13. Spoon about 2 teaspoons of the remaining cream sauce into each pepper.
14. Transfer the peppers to a baking pan and pour the remainder of the tomato sauce into the bottom of the pan.
15. Place the tops back on the peppers and stick them in the oven for 20 minutes.
16. Remove the baking pan from the oven, cover the peppers with aluminium foil.
17. Place the baking pan back in the oven and cook for an additional 30 minutes.
18. Remove the baking pan from the oven, discard the aluminium foil, and garnish with the remaining basil.
19. Place 2 peppers on each plate, serve with a glass of wine, and enjoy!

Chicken Paillard with Grilled Vegetables

Servings| 4   Time| 30 minutes
Nutritional Content (per serving):
Cal| 250   Fat| 11 g   Protein| 31 g   Carbs| 1 g

Ingredients:

- ❖ 4 chicken breast boneless, skinless about 170g each)
- ❖ 1 garlic clove
- ❖ 1/3 tbsp fresh rosemary (chopped)
- ❖ 1/4 tsp salt
- ❖ 1/8 tsp pepper
- ❖ 30 ml lemon juice
- ❖ 30 ml olive oil
- ❖ Grilled vegetable medley (as desired)
- ❖ 4 sprigs fresh rosemary

Directions:

1. Place your chicken breasts between 2 sheets of plastic film. With a meat mallet, carefully pound to about 6 mm.
2. Combine the rosemary, garlic, pepper, and salt. Rub the flattened chicken on both sides with the mixture.
3. Sprinkle both sides with the lemon juice, then with the olive oil. Let marinate 2-4 hours in the refrigerator.
4. Preheat a grill or broiler to very hot. Place the chicken breasts and veggies on the grill or under your broiler, skin side (that is, the side that had the skin on) down, and grill until about one-fourth has done.
5. Rotate on the grill to mark. Continue to cook until about half has done. Turnover and continue to grill until just cooked through.
6. Plate and serve. Garnish with a sprig of rosemary.

Greek- Style Turkey Burgers

Servings| 4   Time| 20 minutes
Nutritional Content (per serving):
Cal|295   Fat| 8 g   Protein| 34 g   Carbs| 23 g

Ingredients:

- ❖ 30 grams finely chopped red onion
- ❖ 30 grams crumbled feta cheese
- ❖ ½ tsp dried oregano
- ❖ 455 grams ground turkey breast
- ❖ 1 tsp salt
- ❖ Freshly ground black pepper
- ❖ 1 tbsp extra-virgin olive oil
- ❖ 110 grams plain non-fat Greek yogurt
- ❖ 1 tbsp chopped fresh mint
- ❖ 1 garlic clove minced
- ❖ 4 whole-wheat hamburger buns
- ❖ Cucumber slices, for serving
- ❖ Tomato slices, for serving
- ❖ Lettuce leaves, for serving

Directions:

1. In a small bowl, stir together the onion, feta, and oregano until well combined.
2. Form the ground turkey into 4 patties and use a spoon to make an indent in the centre of each.
3. Place 2 tablespoons of the feta mixture in the indent in each patty. Fold the edges of the burgers over the filling, pressing to enclose, and flatten the burgers. Season the patties with ½ teaspoon of the salt and some pepper.
4. In a large skillet over medium heat, heat the olive oil.
5. Add the burgers, and cook for 5 minutes per side, flipping once, until browned and cooked through.
6. In a small bowl, whisk the yogurt, mint, garlic, and the remaining ½ teaspoon of salt.
7. Serve the burgers on the buns, topped with a dollop of the yogurt as well as the cucumber, tomato, and lettuce slices.

Chicken Breast and Veggie Bake

Servings| 4   Time| 40 minutes
Nutritional Content (per serving):
Cal|242   Fat| 9 g   Protein| 30 g   Carbs| 12 g

Ingredients:

- 60 ml red wine vinegar
- 2 tbsp extra-virgin olive oil
- 1 tsp fresh thyme or ½ tsp dried thyme
- ½ tsp salt
- Freshly ground black pepper

- 450 grams boneless skinless chicken breasts halved lengthwise
- 1 head broccoli separated into florets
- 1 red bell pepper cut into strips
- 1 red onion cut into wedges
- 230 grams cremini mushrooms

Directions:

1. Preheat the oven to 200 °C (400 °F). Line a baking sheet with parchment paper. Set aside. In a small bowl, whisk the vinegar, olive oil, thyme, salt, and some pepper.
2. Place the chicken in a shallow dish, and pour half of the marinade over the chicken, flipping it to coat.
3. In a large bowl, toss the broccoli, red bell pepper, red onion, and mushrooms with the remaining marinade, being sure to coat all the vegetables.
4. Transfer the vegetables to the prepared baking sheet. Place the chicken breasts on top of the vegetables and pour any remaining marinade over the chicken and vegetables.
5. Bake for 20 to 25 minutes, depending on the thickness of the chicken breasts, until the chicken is cooked through and measures 70 °C on an instant-read thermometer.
6. Serve the chicken with the vegetables.

Mushroom and Beef Burgers

Servings|4 Time| 30 minutes
Nutritional Content (per serving):
Cal| 311   Fat|13 g   Protein| 21 g   Carbs| 29 g

Ingredients:

- ❖ 225 grams cremini mushrooms
- ❖ 1 tbsp extra-virgin olive oil
- ❖ 1 chopped onion finely
- ❖ 3 garlic cloves minced
- ❖ 225 grams lean ground beef
- ❖ ½ tsp salt
- ❖ ¼ tsp freshly ground black pepper
- ❖ 4 whole-wheat hamburger buns
- ❖ Ketchup, for serving
- ❖ Mustard, for serving
- ❖ Lettuce leaves, for serving

Directions:

1. In a food processer, pulse the mushrooms a few times until coarsely ground. Heat the olive oil n a large skillet on medium heat.
2. Add the ground mushrooms, onion, and garlic, and sauté for 8 to 10 minutes, until the vegetables soften, and the liquid evaporates.
3. Remove from the pan, and cool completely. In a large bowl, combine the ground beef, cooled mushroom mixture, salt, and pepper. Mix well.
4. Form the meat mixture into 4 patties. Return the skillet to medium-high heat. Add the patties, and cook for 3 to 5 minutes per side, until cooked to your desired level of doneness.
5. Serve on the buns, topped with ketchup, mustard, and lettuce leaves.

Herb- Crusted Pork Tenderloin

Servings| 4 Time| 35 minutes
Nutritional Content (per serving):
Cal| 301   Fat| 13 g   Protein| 26 g   Carbs| 21 g

Ingredients:

- 1 teaspoon ground mustard
- 1 teaspoon salt
- ½ teaspoon freshly ground black pepper
- 1 (1-pound) pork tenderloin, trimmed
- 2 tablespoons extra-virgin olive oil, divided
- 50 grams whole-wheat panko breadcrumbs
- 2 teaspoons minced fresh thyme
- 1 clove of garlic, minced
- ½ teaspoon ground cumin
- 1 tablespoon Dijon mustard

Directions:

1. Preheat the oven to 220 °C (425 °F). In a small bowl, stir together the dry mustard, salt, and pepper, and rub the spices over the tenderloin.
2. In a large cast iron skillet on medium heat, set 1 tablespoon of olive oil to get hot.
3. Add the pork and sear on all sides, about 2 minutes per side, until browned. Meanwhile, in a small bowl, stir together the breadcrumbs, thyme, garlic, cumin, and remaining 1 tablespoon of olive oil.
4. Spread the mustard on the top of the tenderloin and press the bread crumb mixture into it.
5. Transfer the skillet to the oven and bake for 12 to 15 minutes, until the internal temperature measures 60 °C (160 °F) on an instant-read thermometer and the juices run clear.
6. Let rest for 5 minutes before slicing and serving.

Flank Steak with Chimichurri

Servings| 4   Time| 25 minutes
Nutritional Content (per serving):
Cal| 263   Fat| 17 g   Protein| 25 g   Carbs| 1 g

Ingredients:
For The Chimichurri:
- 15 grams packed fresh parsley leaves
- 15 grams packed fresh coriander leaves
- 30 grams chopped red onion
- 1 garlic clove, peeled
- 2 tablespoons extra-virgin olive oil
- 2 tablespoons water

- 1 tablespoon apple cider vinegar
- ¼ teaspoon salt
- Freshly ground black pepper
- Red pepper flakes

For The Flank Steak:
- 1 pound flank steak, trimmed
- 1 teaspoon salt
- ½ teaspoon garlic powder
- Freshly ground black pepper

Directions:
To Make the Chimichurri:
1. In a food processor, combine the parsley, coriander, red onion, garlic, olive oil, water, vinegar, and salt.
2. Pulse a few times until just combined. Season with red pepper flakes, and black pepper then set aside.

To Make the Flank Steak
3. Season both sides of the steak with the salt, garlic powder, and some black pepper.
4. Heat a large cast iron skillet over high heat.
5. Add the steak to the hot pan, and cook for 3 to 5 minutes per side, flipping once, until medium-rare.
6. Transfer to a cutting board and let rest for 5 minutes. Cut into thin strips across the grain and serve topped with the chimichurri sauce.

Rosemary- Crusted Lamb

Servings| 4   Time| 25 minutes
Nutritional Content (per serving):
Cal| 396   Fat| 29 g   Protein| 30 g   Carbs| 1 g

Ingredients:

- ❖ 3 garlic cloves, minced
- ❖ 2 tablespoons extra-virgin olive oil
- ❖ 2 teaspoons chopped fresh rosemary
- ❖ 1 teaspoon salt
- ❖ ½ teaspoon freshly ground black pepper
- ❖ 900 grams lamb rib chops, trimmed

Directions:

1. In a small bowl, stir together the garlic, olive oil, rosemary, salt, and pepper. Spread the mixture onto the lamb chops and let rest for 30 minutes.
2. Heat a large cast iron skillet over medium-high heat. Press the rosemary and garlic onto the chops, and, working in batches, gently place the chops in the hot pan.
3. Cook for 4 to 5 minutes per side, flipping once, until medium-rare. Keep warm while cooking the remaining chops and serve.

Cherry Barbecue Chicken Cutlets

Servings| 4   Time| 15 minutes
Nutritional Content (per serving):
Cal| 272   Fat| 6 g   Protein| 40 g   Carbs| 16 g

Ingredients:

- ❖ 700 grams boneless, skinless chicken cutlets
- ❖ Cherry Barbecue Sauce, store-bought, divided
- ❖ 1½ tablespoons extra-virgin olive oil

Directions:

1. Marinate the chicken in half the barbecue sauce in the refrigerator for up to 1 day.
2. The following day, heat the extra-virgin olive oil in a large skillet over high heat. Add the cutlets and cook without disturbing them. Make sure they do not touch, about 1 to 2 inches apart. Cook until brown, 2 to 3 minutes. Flip, and cook another 30 seconds.
3. Repeat with the remaining chicken cutlets if they do not all fit in one pan without overcrowding.
4. Allow the chicken to rest for 5 minutes before serving.
5. Meanwhile, heat the remaining sauce in a small saucepan, then serve with the cooked chicken.

Herbed Buttermilk Chicken

Servings| 4   Time| 30 minutes
Nutritional Content (per serving):
Cal| 437   Fat| 20 g   Protein| 46 g   Carbs| 19 g

Ingredients:

- 680 grams boneless
- 950 ml buttermilk
- Pinch kosher salt
- Pinch freshly ground black pepper
- 115 grams thinly sliced yellow onion
- 2 tbsp canola oil
- 9 grams Italian seasoning
- 1 lemon cut into wedges

Directions:

1. In a large bowl or sealable plastic bag, combine the chicken, buttermilk, salt, and pepper. Cover or seal and refrigerate for at least 1 hour and up to 24 hours.
2. When the chicken is ready to cook, preheat the oven to 220 °C (425 °F). Line a baking sheet with parchment paper.
3. Remove the chicken from the buttermilk brine and pat it dry. Place the chicken on the prepared baking sheet along with the onion, and drizzle everything with the canola oil.
4. Toss together on the baking sheet (this will save you a bowl) to coat the chicken and onion evenly.
5. Bake for 25 minutes or until the chicken is cooked through. (If the chicken is thick, you can cut the breasts in half lengthwise.
6. It will cut down on your cook time by half or less. Check the chicken after it's cooked for 8 minutes if the breasts are thin.)
7. Allow the chicken to rest and sprinkle it and the onions with the Italian seasoning.
8. Serve with a squeeze of lemon juice.

Dessert

Sweet-Baked Banana

Servings| 5   Time| 35 minutes
Nutritional Content (per serving):
Cal| 181   Fat| 1 g   Protein| 2 g   Carbs| 48 g

Ingredients:
- ❖ 6 ripe bananas
- ❖ 4 tbsp honey

- ❖ 3 ¾ tsp cinnamon

Directions:
1. Preheat oven to 180 °C (350 °F). Slice bananas into bite-sized chunks.
2. Pour honey and cinnamon into a medium-sized bowl. Mix until cinnamon is evenly spread through the honey.
3. Add bananas and gently toss until they have an even coating.
4. Transfer bananas onto a lined baking sheet. Spread them into one even layer.
5. Place the baking sheet into the oven and bake for 10-15 minutes or until bananas are slightly browned.
6. Portion into 2 bowls and enjoy!

Banana Pudding with Meringue

Servings| 10   Time| 50 minutes
Nutritional Content (per serving):
Cal| 324   Fat| 14 g   Protein| 42 g   Carbs| 12 g

Ingredients:

For the Pudding:
- ❖ 180 ml erythritol
- ❖ 5 tsp almond flour
- ❖ Salt
- ❖ 600 ml fat-free milk
- ❖ 6 tbsp prepared egg replacement
- ❖ Vanilla extract.)

- ❖ 2 (230 grams) Spelt hazelnut biscuits containers honey-free, crushed)
- ❖ 5 bananas (sliced)

For the Meringue:
- ❖ 5 medium egg whites
- ❖ 80 ml erythritol
- ❖ ½ tsp vanilla extract

Directions:

To Make the Pudding
1. In a saucepan, whisk the erythritol, almond flour, salt, and milk together. Cook over medium heat until the honey is dissolved.
2. Whisk in the egg replacement and cook for about 10 minutes, or until thickened.
3. Remove from the heat and stir in the vanilla. Spread the thickened pudding onto the bottom of a casserole dish.
4. Arrange a layer of crushed biscuits on top of the pudding. Place a layer of sliced bananas on top of the biscuits.

To Make the Meringue
1. Preheat the oven to 180 °C (350 °F). In a medium bowl, beat the egg whites for about 5 minutes, or until stiff.
2. Add the erythritol and vanilla while continuing to beat for about 3 more minutes.
3. Spread the meringue on top of the banana pudding.
4. Transfer the casserole dish to the oven, and bake for 7 to 10 minutes, or until the top is lightly browned.

Walnut Crescent Cookies

Servings| 10   Time| 70 minutes
Nutritional Content (per serving):
Cal| 408   Fat| 30 g   Protein| 6 g   Carbs| 30 g

Ingredients:
Dough:
- ❖ Whole wheat flour (470g)
- ❖ Corn oil (2 ⅓ dl)
- ❖ Dry white wine (1 ⅛ dl)
- ❖ Honey (70g)

Filling:
- ❖ Walnuts (250g, diced)
- ❖ Apple (1, shredded)
- ❖ Honey (2 tbsp.)
- ❖ Whole wheat breadcrumbs (2 tbsp.)
- ❖ Strawberry jam (1 tbsp.)
- ❖ Cinnamon (½ tsp.)
- ❖ Honey for dusting

Directions:
1. Put the corn oil and honey in a large bowl and stir together until well combined.
2. Add the dry white wine and whole wheat flour. Beat this in until a dough is formed.
3. Once dough forms, remove it from the bowl and knead it over a flat surface until soft, but not sticky. Then, let the dough sit for 30 minutes.
4. While the dough sits, you can begin to prepare the filling. Start by putting the walnuts, apple, honey, whole wheat breadcrumbs, strawberry jam, and cinnamon in a large bowl.
5. Mix all the ingredients until well combined. Set aside. Preheat oven to 180 °C (350 °F).
6. Once half of an hour has passed, flatten the dough out over a floured flat surface until it is 5 mm thick.
7. Using a glass cup, cut circles out of the dough.
8. Set the circles aside, roll the remaining dough out again and repeat step 7 until little or no dough is left.
9. Once all of your dough has been cut into circles, divide the filling between them, dolloping a little bit in the centre of each.
10. Fold each circle in half over the top of the filling and squish the edges nicely into one another so that none of the filling can seep out.
11. Line a baking sheet with parchment paper and spread the crescents out over the top.
12. Place the baking sheet in the oven and let the crescents bake for 20 minutes.
13. After 20 minutes, remove the baking sheet from the oven. Dust with Honey.

Orange Bundt Cake

Servings| 24   Time| 45 minutes
Nutritional Content (per serving):
Cal| 180   Fat| 12 g   Protein| 4 g   Carbs| 15 g

Ingredients:

- Unsalted non-hydrogenated plant-based butter, for greasing the pan
- 350 grams gluten-free, (plus more for dusting) baking flour
- 350 grams almond flour
- ½ tsp baking soda
- ½ tsp baking powder
- 9 medium eggs (at room temperature)
- 220 grams coconut honey
- Zest of 3 oranges
- Juice of 1 orange
- 230 ml extra-virgin olive oil

Directions:

1. Preheat the oven to 160 °C (325 °F). Grease two Bundt pans with butter and dust with the baking flour.
2. In a medium bowl, whisk the baking flour, almond flour, baking soda, and baking powder together.
3. In a large bowl, whip the eggs with the coconut honey until they double in size.
4. Add the orange zest and orange juice. Add the dry ingredients to the wet ingredients, stirring to combine.
5. Add the olive oil, a little at a time, until incorporated. Divide the batter between the two prepared Bundt pans.
6. Transfer the Bundt pans to the oven, and bake for 30 minutes, or until browned and a toothpick inserted into the centre comes out clean.
7. Remove the Bundt pans from the oven and let cool for 15 minutes.
8. Invert the Bundt pans onto plates, and gently tap the cakes out of the pan.

Traditional Ekmek Kataifi

Servings| 12   Time| 110 minutes
Nutritional Content (per serving):
Cal| 367   Fat| 20 g   Protein| 6 g   Carbs| 45 g

Ingredients:
Pastry:
- ❖ 230 grams kataifi dough
- ❖ 80 grams pistachios (diced)
- ❖ 110 ml olive oil

Syrup:
- ❖ 180 ml water
- ❖ 180 grams honey
- ❖ 110 grams cinnamon
- ❖ 80 ml strawberry puree

- ❖ ½ tbsp lemon zest

Custard:
- ❖ 720 ml milk
- ❖ 150 grams honey
- ❖ 80 ml olive oil
- ❖ 80 ml corn starch
- ❖ 4 egg yolks
- ❖ ½ tsp vanilla extract

Directions:
1. Preheat oven to 170 ºC (325 ºF). Knead the Kataifi dough, spreading apart the clumped together strands to create a fluffier consistency.
2. Spray a baking dish with cooking spray and press the Kataifi dough into the bottom of it, forming one even layer.
3. Pour the olive oil over the top and place the baking dish in the oven for 30-40 minutes, or until it is light brown.
4. While the Kataifi is in the oven, you can begin to prepare your custard. Start by placing half of the honey and all the egg yolks in a bowl, whisking them together until well combined and bubbly. Set the mixture aside for later.
5. In a separate bowl, whisk together 4 tbsp. of milk and the corn starch until well combined. Set this mixture aside for later as well.
6. Pour the remaining milk into a large non-stick pan over high heat along with the honey and vanilla extract.
7. Stir this together well and bring the mixture to a boil. Remove the pan from the heat as soon as the milk begins to boil. Set aside.
8. Pour 1/3 of the pan's mixture into the egg yolk mixture and whisk it in until well combined.
9. Transfer the egg yolk mixture back into the pan and place the pan back overheat, but this time on medium.
10. Whisk continuously while cooking is in progress until the mixture becomes all thick, smooth, and deliciously creamy.

12. Once the mixture is thick and rich, remove it again from the heat.
13. Add the olive oil to the pan and stir it into the mixture until melted and well combined.
14. Transfer this mixture into a baking tray and place some plastic wrap over the top of it. Ensure the plastic wrap touches the mixture to ensure it stays creamy.
15. Set this aside, let it cool, and while you're going strong, begin to prepare the syrup.
16. Stir the water, honey, strawberry puree, lemon zest, and cinnamon stick together in a small pot or saucepan over medium heat until the honey has dissolved.
17. Bring the mixture to a boil and let it boil for 3 minutes until it thickens into a syrup consistency.
18. Once it's thick enough, remove it from the heat and let it cool until it's just warm enough for you to eat it without burning your mouth.
19. By now your Kataifi dough should have been removed from the oven and cooled. If this is not the case, wait until it is cool.
20. Once the Kataifi is cool, ladle the syrup over the top one at a time, giving each spoonful enough time to be absorbed. Then, set it aside to cool completely.
21. Spread the creamy custard atop the Kataifi in a nice, even layer.
22. Sprinkle the chopped pistachios over the entire thing. You can be as creative as you like!
23. Make a smiley face or a rainbow to impress your friends.
24. Slice into 12 pieces, serve, and enjoy!

Flaky Coconut Pie

Servings| 12   Time| 75 minutes
Nutritional Content (per serving):
Cal| 385   Fat| 28 g   Protein| 6 g   Carbs| 31 g

Ingredients:
- 11 sheets filo pastry
- 400 ml coconut cream
- 110 grams cashew (chopped)
- 110 grams honey
- 80 grams coconut oil
- 80 grams coconut (shredded, unsweetened)
- 2 eggs
- 1 tsp vanilla extract

Directions:
1. reheat oven to 180 °C (350 °F). Grease a pie dish with just enough coconut oil to cover it.
2. In a medium-size bowl, whisk together the coconut cream, honey, eggs, and vanilla until all ingredients are well combined and the honey has dissolved. Set this aside for later.
3. Pulse the cashews and shredded coconut in a food processor until it turns into mulch. Set this aside as well.
4. Place a piece of the filo pastry on a clean, stable surface and brush a generous amount of coconut oil over it.
5. Roughly scrunch the piece of filo pastry up and place it in the pie dish. Repeat steps 5-6 until the baking tray is full.
6. Once your pie dish is full, pour the coconut cream mixture over top, making sure each inch of the pastry gets soaked in it.
7. Once you're out of your coconut cream mixture, sprinkle the cashew mixture over top.
8. Place the pie dish in the oven and let it bake for 25-35 minutes or until the top has turned a nice golden-brown and the pastry has risen.
9. Remove the baking tray from the oven and allow your pie to cool for 15 minutes.
10. Slice into 8 wedges and enjoy!

Ricotta Cheese Fruit Bake

Servings| 6   Time| 100 minutes
Nutritional Content (per serving):
Cal| 153   Fat| 6 g   Protein| 6 g   Carbs| 19 g

Ingredients:
Ricotta Cheese:
- ❖ 350 grams ricotta cheese
- ❖ 1 egg
- ❖ 3 tbsp honey
- ❖ 1 tsp lemon zest

Fruit Syrup:
- ❖ 250 grams raspberries (diced)
- ❖ 3 tbsp honey
- ❖ 2 tbsp orange juice
- ❖ 1 tsp orange blossom water

Directions:
1. Place ricotta cheese in a coffee filter-lined strainer and place this in the fridge to drain overnight.
2. Ensure the filter is placed over a container so that the drained mixture is contained.
3. Once your ricotta cheese has drained, preheat the oven to 200 °C. Spray 6 small heat-proof bowls with cooking spray.
4. Place the drained ricotta, egg, honey, and lemon in a bowl and beat together until well combined.
5. Divide the ricotta mixture between your 6 greased bowls and place them in the oven for 30-35 minutes, or until they have turned a nice golden-brown colour.
6. Then, remove them from the oven and allow them to cool. While your ricotta cheese bowls are cooling, you can begin to prepare the fruit sauce.
7. Start by placing the raspberries, honey, and orange juice in a small pot or saucepan over medium-high heat.
8. As it starts to boil, stir so that ingredients are well combined and the honey dissolves.
9. Once the mixture starts to boil, reduce the heat to medium-low and continue to cook, stirring occasionally, for 20-25 minutes or until the raspberries are tender and the mixture takes on a syrupy consistency.
10. Remove the mixture from the heat and stir in the orange blossom water until well combined. Then, let the mixture cool a little.
11. Once the ricotta cheese bowls have cooled, divide the fruit syrup over them.
12. Serve and enjoy!

Anginetti Lemon Cookies

Servings| 12   Time| 50 minutes
Nutritional Content (per serving):
Cal| 104   Fat| 3 g   Protein| 1 g   Carbs| 18 g

Ingredients:
Cookies:
- 150 grams whole wheat flour
- 1 egg
- 2 ½ tbsp honey
- 2 tbsp olive oil
- 2/3 tsp baking powder
- 2/3 tsp vanilla extract
- 1/3 tsp lemon zest (grated)

Icing:
- 110 grams honey (sifted)
- 2 tsp lemon juice
- 2 tsp water
- 1 tsp olive oil
- 1/3 tsp vanilla extract

Directions:
1. Preheat oven to 180 ºC (350 ºF). Prepare a baking sheet by lining it with foil.
2. Start with the cookies. Beat together the honey, olive oil, vanilla extract, and lemon zest together until ingredients are well combined.
3. Crack the egg into the mixture and beat it in as well. Then, set this mixture aside for later.
4. In a separate bowl, stir together the whole wheat flour and baking powder until well combined.
5. Gradually add this to the wet mixture, beating it in as you go.
6. Once your cookie dough is smooth and lump-free, begin to dollop it out onto the lined baking sheet. You should be able to get 12 cookies out of the mixture.
7. Place the baking sheet into the oven and bake for 10-12 minutes or until they become a nice golden-brown colour.
8. While the cookies are in the oven, you can begin to prepare the icing. Start by putting the olive oil in a small pot or saucepan over medium heat.
9. Once the oil has heated, add in the honey, lemon juice, water, and vanilla extract, stirring ingredients into the oil until well combined. Add a little more water to the icing if it seems too thick.
10. Once the cookies are done, brush the lemon icing over the top while they're still hot.
11. After you have applied the icing, allow the cookies to cool.
12. Once the cookies are cool, serve, and enjoy!

Banana, Peach, and Almond Fritters

Servings| 7   Time| 30 minutes
Nutritional Content (per serving):
Cal| 163   Fat| 7 g   Protein| 6 g   Carbs| 22 g

Ingredients:

- 4 ripe, peeled bananas
- 470 grams peaches (chopped)
- 1 egg
- 2 egg whites
- 180 grams almond meal
- ¼ tsp almond extract

Directions:

1. In a large bowl, mash the bananas and peaches together with a fork or potato masher.
2. Blend in the egg and egg whites. Stir in the almond meal and almond extract.
3. ⅔-dl portions of the batter into the basket of an air fryer. Set the air fryer to 200 °C (400 °F). Close, and cook for 12 minutes.
4. Once cooking is complete, transfer the fritters to a plate. Repeat until no batter remains.

Chocolate Cheesecake Mousse

Servings| 4   Time| 10 minutes
Nutritional Content (per serving):
Cal| 83   Fat| 5 g   Protein| 3 g   Carbs| 7 g

Ingredients:

- ❖ 1 tbsp semisweet chocolate chips
- ❖ 180 grams Non-fat Whipped Milk Base (see recipe in this chapter), divided
- ❖ 30 grams cream cheese
- ❖ 11 /2 tsp cocoa
- ❖ 1 tsp vanilla extract

Directions:

1. Put chocolate chips and 1 tablespoon of Non-fat Whipped Milk Base in microwave-safe bowl and microwave on high for 15 seconds.
2. Add cream cheese and microwave on high for another 15 seconds. Whip mixture until well blended and chocolate chips are melted.
3. Stir in cocoa and vanilla. Fold in remaining Non-fat Whipped Milk Base. Chill until ready to serve.

Whipped Lemon Cheesecake Mousse

Servings| 10   Time| 10 minutes
Nutritional Content (per serving):
Cal| 81   Fat| 4 g   Protein| 4 g   Carbs|8 g

Ingredients:

- ❖ 110 grams cream cheese
- ❖ 1 tbsp lemon juice
- ❖ 1 tsp lemon zest

- ❖ 30 grams powdered sugar
- ❖ 1 recipe Non-fat Whipped Milk Base (see recipe in this chapter)

Directions:

1. In a small bowl, combine cream cheese, lemon juice, lemon zest, and sugar. Using fork or whisk, beat until well blended.
2. Fold mixture into Whipped Milk Base. Chill for at least 1 hour before serving.

Non-fat Whipped Milk Base

Servings|3 cups   Time|15 minutes
Nutritional Content (per serving):
Cal| 290   Fat|1 g   Protein| 28 g   Carbs|42 g

Ingredients:

- ❖ 20 grams non-fat milk powder
- ❖ 20 grams powdered sugar
- ❖ 250 ml chilled skim milk, divided
- ❖ 1½ envelopes Knox Original Unflavoured Gelatine

Directions:

Whipping Methods:

1. Because you don't need to whip the Non-fat Whipped Milk Base until it reaches stiff peaks, you can use a blender or food processor; however, you won't be whipping as much air into the mixture if you do, so the serving sizes will be a bit smaller.
2. In a chilled bowl, combine milk powder and sugar; mix until well blended. Pour 60 ml milk and gelatine into blender. Let sit for 1–2 minutes to allow gelatine to soften.
3. In microwave-safe container, heat remaining milk on high until it almost reaches boiling point, 30–45 seconds.
4. Add milk to blender with gelatine; blend 2 minutes, or until gelatine is completely dissolved. Chill for 15 minutes, or until mixture is cool but gelatine hasn't yet begun to set.
5. Using your whisk or hand mixer, beat until the mixture doubles in size. (It won't make stiff peaks like you would get from whipped cream but it will become creamier in colour.)
6. Chill until ready to use in desserts. If necessary, whip again immediately prior to folding in other ingredients.

Peach Bread Pudding

Servings|9   Time| 55 minutes
Nutritional Content (per serving):
Cal| 164   Fat| 5 g   Protein| 7 g   Carbs| 23 g

Ingredients:

- ❖ Non-stick cooking spray
- ❖ 500 ml 1% milk
- ❖ 2 tablespoons butter
- ❖ 2 eggs
- ❖ 80.19 grams egg whites
- ❖ 1 teaspoon vanilla extract
- ❖ 2 teaspoons cinnamon
- ❖ 2 Tbsp + 2 tsp Splenda Brown Sugar Blend
- ❖ 6 slices whole-wheat bread, cubed
- ❖ 500 grams sliced peaches

Directions:

1. Preheat oven to 180 °C (350 °F). Spray baking dish with non-stick cooking spray.
2. Heat milk in a small saucepan over low heat. Melt butter in milk. Cool.
3. In a medium bowl, beat eggs, egg whites, vanilla, cinnamon, and Splenda.
4. Combine milk and egg mixtures.
5. Place cubed bread in an even layer in prepared baking dish. Place sliced peaches on top of bread cubes.
6. Pour egg mixture over bread and peaches. Bake for 40–45 minutes.

Fruit Compote

Servings| 4   Time| 15 minutes
Nutritional Content (per serving):
Cal| 117   Fat|2 g   Protein| 1 g   Carbs| 24 g

Ingredients:
- ❖ 230 grams chopped apples
- ❖ 2 tablespoons dried cranberries
- ❖ 6 dried apricots, diced
- ❖ 1/4 teaspoon cinnamon
- ❖ 2 tablespoons water
- ❖ 1 tablespoon brandy (optional; if not used, add additional 3 tablespoons water)
- ❖ 1 tablespoon finely chopped walnuts

Directions:
1. In a small saucepan, combine apples, cranberries, apricots, cinnamon, water, and brandy.
2. Cook over medium heat until apples are softened, about 10 minutes. Remove from heat and cover 5 minutes. Stir in walnuts before serving.

Meringue Pie Crust

Servings| 9 inch pie crust   Time| 3-4 hours
Nutritional Content (per serving):
Cal| 94   Fat| 5 g   Protein| 3 g   Carbs| 10 g

Ingredients:

- Non-stick cooking spray, as needed
- 4 egg whites
- Pinch salt
- 1 teaspoon vinegar
- 3½ teaspoons cup sugar substitute, or to taste
- 50 grams toasted walnuts, hazelnuts, or pecans

Directions:

1. Prepare a pan with non-stick cooking spray.
2. In a medium bowl, beat egg whites by adding salt and then vinegar and sugar substitute. When stiff, fold in nuts.
3. Pile into pie pan. Bake at 80 °C (160 °F) for 3–4 hours.
4. Let cool before filling. The meringue should be used the same day it's made and served immediately after it's filled. Once filled or sitting out in a humid room, it will turn soggy.

Strawberry Rhubarb Cobbler

Servings| 9   Time| 50 minutes
Nutritional Content (per serving):
Cal| 138   Fat| 3 g   Protein| 3 g   Carbs| 27 g

Ingredients:

- ❖ Non - stick cooking spray
- ❖ 480 grams chopped rhubarb
- ❖ 335 grams thickly sliced strawberries
- ❖ ¼ tsp lemon zest
- ❖ 110 grams sugar
- ❖ 4 tbsp Splenda Granulated
- ❖ 2 tbsp corn starch
- ❖ 2 tbsp water
- ❖ 80 grams whole-wheat pastry flour
- ❖ ¼ tsp ground ginger
- ❖ 1½ tsp baking powder
- ❖ ½ tsp salt
- ❖ 2½ tbsp canola oil
- ❖ 2 tbsp milk
- ❖ 2 tbsp egg whites

Directions:

1. Preheat oven to 190 °C (375 °F). Spray baking dish with non-stick cooking spray.
2. In a mixing bowl, combine rhubarb, strawberries, lemon zest, sugar, and Splenda.
3. In a small bowl, dissolve corn starch in water. Pour over fruit and stir to coat. Place in prepared baking dish and set aside.
4. In a small bowl, sift together 1 tablespoon sugar, flour, ginger, baking powder, and salt. Add oil, milk, and egg whites; stir quickly until just mixed.
5. Drop dough by spoonful over fruit. If desired, loosely spread dough over fruit. Bake for 25–30 minutes, until dough is golden brown.

Baked Pear Crisp

Servings| 4   Time| 50 minutes
Nutritional Content (per serving):
Cal| 200   Fat| 4 g   Protein| 2 g   Carbs| 42 g

Ingredients:

- 2 pears
- 2 tablespoons frozen unsweetened pineapple juice concentrate
- 1 teaspoon vanilla extract
- 1 teaspoon dark rum

- 1 tablespoon butter
- 20 grams Ener-G Brown Rice Flour
- 55 grams firmly packed brown sugar
- 25 grams oat bran flakes

Directions:

1. Preheat oven to 190 °C (375 °F). Treat baking dish or large flat casserole dish with non-stick cooking spray. Core and cut up pears; place in baking dish. (Except for any bruised spots, it's okay to leave skins on.)
2. In a small microwave-safe bowl, microwave frozen juice concentrate for 1 minute. Stir in vanilla and rum and pour over pears.
3. Using same bowl, microwave butter 30–40 seconds, until melted; set aside.
4. Toss remaining ingredients in a separate bowl, being careful not to crush cereal.
5. Spread uniformly over pears. Drizzle melted butter over top. Bake for 35 minutes, or until mixture is bubbling and top is just beginning to brown.
6. Serve hot or cold.

Thank you for going through the book, I sincerely hope you enjoyed the recipes.

As I said before, a lot of time went into creating so many recipes and I really hope you are satisfied with the recipes provided.

I am trying really hard to create the best recipes I can and I am always open to feedback so whether you liked or disliked the book feel free to write on my email at deliciousrecipes.publishing@gmail.com. I always reply and love to communicate with everybody. If you did not like the recipes you can reach out and I will share another cookbook or two for free in order to try to improve your experience at least a little bit.

Thank you for going through the recipes, enjoy!

Printed in Great Britain
by Amazon

83581007R00068